LANDS and PEOPLES

SPECIAL EDITION: LIFE AFTER COMMUNISM

GROLIER

LANDS and
PEOPLES

SPECIAL EDITION:
LIFE AFTER COMMUNISM

STAFF

Lawrence T. Lorimer . . . . .Editorial Director
Joseph M. Castagno . . . . .Executive Editor
Lisa Holland . . . . .Editor
Doris E. Lechner . . . . .Director, Annuals
Irina Rybacek .Text Author
Elizabeth Farrington . . . . .Art Director
Meghan O'Reilly LeBlanc . . . . .Copy Editor
Stephan M. Romanoff . . . . .Proofreader
Karen A. Fairchild . . . . .Editorial Assistant
Jeffrey H. Hacker . . . . .Managing Editor
Ann Eriksen . . . . .Chief, Photo Research
Paula K. Wehde . . . . .Photo Researcher
Jane H. Carruth . . . . .Manager, Picture Library
Lyndee Stalter . . . . .Production Assistant
Pauline M. Sholtys . . . . .Chief Indexer
Linda King . . . . .Indexer
Joseph J. Corlett . . . . .Director of Manufacturing
Christine L. Matta . . . . .Senior Production Manager
Pamela J. Terwilliger . . . . .Production Manager
Gailynn French . . . . .Production Assistant

ISBN 0-7172-8017-9

Printed in the United States of America

Contents

The Fall of
Communism   2

A Year-by-Year
Overview   16

An Alphabetical
Overview   50

Looking toward
the next century   100

Index   106

Illustration credits   108

The crowds that brought down the Communist regimes throughout Eastern Europe must now build up strong democratic governments. In many places, however, this process has been derailed by ethnic violence.

The Fall of Communism

By late 1992, the once-mighty Communist empire had been shattered into pieces. The Soviet Union, for seven decades the bastion of Marxist ideology, had been replaced by a loose alliance called the Commonwealth of Independent States. Ethnic violence in Transcaucasia, feeding on centuries-old animosities, had claimed hundreds of lives, and a conflict between old-time Communist forces and a coalition of democrats and Islamic groups in Tajikistan in Central Asia began to resemble a civil war. Every former Soviet republic was beset by economic hardships and a host of new uncertainties.

In central and southern Europe, the former Communist states were grappling with the challenges of post-Communism: economic, political, and social transformation of their systems on the one hand and the reappearance of old national rivalries on the other. Yugoslavia, once a showcase of a liberal, seemingly benevolent "third way" hybrid between a democratic and Communist system, had disintegrated into a brutal battlefield. Indeed, post-Communist Yugoslavia has seen the most ferocious fighting on European soil since World War II, replete with such ominous phenomena as concentration camps and "ethnic cleansing." By contrast, Czechoslovakia, for most of the 20th century a common state of Czechs and Slovaks, was peacefully splitting into two countries.

It was not only in Europe that traditional Communism was in decline. China, the giant of Asia, was quite successfully grafting capitalist economic policies onto its Communist politics. In central Asia, Mongolia, although still governed by former Communists, renounced socialism and permitted the reemergence of Buddhism, its traditional religion. North Korea, long the world's most adamantly Communist country, began cautiously opening its doors to the West. Even Vietnam, the long-time adversary of the United States, has grown much more friendly.

At the other end of the world, Fidel Castro in Cuba was desperately trying to maintain his island's hard-line Communist stance. To many observers, however, Castro's actions will ultimately prove to be an exercise in futility.

The most amazing thing about the fall of Communism is how fast it occurred. Indeed, within a mere few years, the world has fundamentally changed—a fact that begs two simple questions: how and why? This book will venture to answer these questions through a multilayered portrayal of what happened in the Soviet Union and Eastern Europe since Mikhail Gorbachev came to power in 1985. First, in the following pages of this introductory section, we will go back in time to look at the origins of Communism and socialism, and to review briefly the tortured history of this movement throughout the 20th century. The next section will discuss the main features of Communist regimes, and the section after that will deal with daily life under Communism. After a brief survey of how the Communist regimes were toppled, the section will close with a consideration of the reasons why Communism failed.

The second part of the book is a Chronology, which traces the developments in the Communist world from 1944 onward. This section is organized in columns, country by country. Until the late 1980s, only the most crucial events are listed; for the past five years, however, the chronology goes month by month. The events for 1992 are presented in two spreads: one for central and eastern Europe and the other for the republics of the former Soviet Union.

The names and terms that are boldfaced in the chronology are the main entries in the third part of the book, the Alphabetical Overview. Approximately 130 entries include all of the former Communist countries and the newly constituted successor states, some important regions, significant personalities, and various terms and organizations. The entries are brief and should serve as a quick orientation only. A much more detailed treatment of individual countries appears in the main volumes of the **LANDS & PEOPLES** set. The concluding section of the book, "Life After Communism—Looking Toward the Next Century," surveys the main problems that arose after the fall of Communist governments and briefly considers the likely future developments in different regions.

Historical Background

Origins of Socialism and Communism. Communist regimes have caused so much suffering in so many parts of the world that all other tyrannies throughout the whole of human history pale in comparison. Ironically, this greatest modern tragedy started with a dream. The words "socialism" and "Communism," dating from the 1830s and 1840s, stood for a vision of a new and better world. Regardless of whether Marx, Lenin, and other founding fathers of this movement were visionaries or power seekers, it is a fact that millions of people in many parts of the world believed, some for a short time and others for their whole lives, that socialism and Communism are the noblest goals of human history—causes worth dying for.

In the middle of the 19th century, German thinker and revolutionary Karl Marx formulated a theory of Communism as the highest stage in history, in which all exploitation and poverty would be abolished, people would work in creative ways, and the state with its powers of repression would vanish. Marx then predicted a world revolution that would usher in socialism—a transitory stage between capitalism and Communism—and the "dictatorship of the proletariat." Although Marx's theory underwent multiple metamorphoses, its promise of equality and justice has proved extremely appealing for more than 100 years.

The Rise of the Soviet Union. When Lenin formed his Bolshevik Party (which became the Communist Party after the October Revolution in 1917), he complemented the original Marxist vision with an important new addition: he made the party the leader of society. Lenin died a few years after the Communists took power, and students of Soviet history still argue whether or not the Soviet regime would have become more benevolent under his leadership had he lived longer. In any case, Lenin's successor, Stalin, created such a malign, evil, and oppressive system that millions of people are still affected by it. The reasons for this are complex and include both Stalin's personality and the legacies of Russian history: Stalin was a man who yearned to be the ultimate ruler, suspicious of everyone, probably full of inferiority complexes (which he compensated for by getting rid of all his real and potential adversaries), and certainly paranoid in his later years. He was at the same time very devious and scheming, able to deceive not only his compatriots but also many Westerners as well. Russian history and society were another important part of the equation: when the Bolsheviks took over, most of the population were illiterate peasants, people for whom the words "democracy" and "freedom" smacked of "anarchy." When these two factors, Stalin and Russia, combined with a theory of state ownership of all means of production and the leading role of the party, the result was the monstrous Stalinist socialism.

Communist Expansion Throughout the World. At a tremendous cost in human lives and with almost unimaginable waste, Stalin managed to transform the Soviet Union from a feudal backward empire into an industrialized mammoth. In 1945, by means of the Yalta agreements with the Western Allied powers, he then laid the groundwork for the post-World War II expansion. In the closing days of the war, the Soviet armies

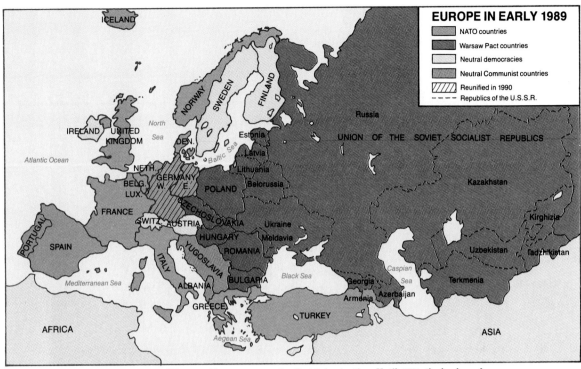

EUROPE IN EARLY 1989

- NATO countries
- Warsaw Pact countries
- Neutral democracies
- Neutral Communist countries
- Reunified in 1990
- Republics of the U.S.S.R.

After World War II, most of Eastern Europe came under Soviet domination. Until 1989, the borders of most of the countries above had remained the same for decades.

By early 1993, Europe looked considerably different. After the Soviet Union collapsed, the Commonwealth of Independent States (CIS) was founded to maintain ties between some former Soviet republics.

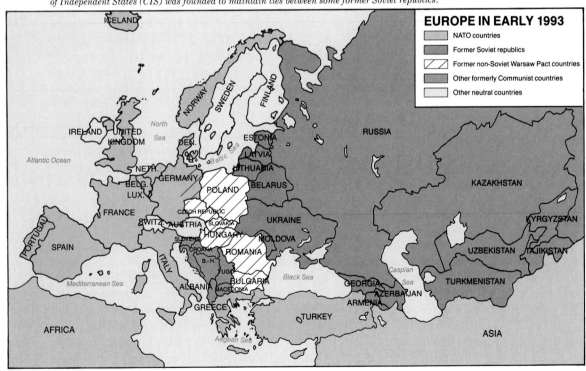

EUROPE IN EARLY 1993

- NATO countries
- Former Soviet republics
- Former non-Soviet Warsaw Pact countries
- Other formerly Communist countries
- Other neutral countries

Soviet tanks propped up the Communist regimes imposed on Eastern Europe after World War II. The threat of further military action helped keep the Communist regimes in the Soviet camp.

advanced west in pursuit of German troops. Ever suspicious of the West, from 1944 onward Stalin went on systematically engineering and promoting Communist takeovers in the Eastern European countries newly occupied by Soviet troops. The mechanism of these takeovers was similar: Communist parties, backed by the U.S.S.R., first allied themselves with other parties, then gradually weakened them, subverted or co-opted them, and finally usurped all power. Two exceptions to this were Yugoslavia and Albania, where strong national leaders appeared during the war: both Josip Broz Tito and Enver Hoxha were guerrilla heroes who commanded genuine respect among the population.

The first period of Communism in Eastern Europe was a somewhat diluted copy of the Stalinist 1930s: expropriation of private property, nationalizations, collectivization of agriculture, abolition of civil liberties, purges of anti-Communist opposition and persecution of "class enemies," show trials, executions, and widespread terror. After these harsh years, Eastern Europe settled into a more lenient stage, which was less explicitly brutal, but in many ways more pernicious.

Meanwhile, Communist regimes also arose in Asia. The second-oldest Communist country in the world, Mongolia, became a "People's Republic" in November 1924. After World War II, China and North Korea joined the Communist world, and, in 1954, North Vietnam followed suit. In 1959, Cuba set out on its Communist adventure, and during the following decade many African governments turned to Marxism. At that time, with Communists controlling the largest country in the world, the most populous country in the world, and scores of smaller nations, it seemed that Communism was indeed marching toward victory.

The Main Characteristics of Communist Societies

The Leading Role of the Party. This was the main contribution of Lenin to the old Marxist theory: the party is the vanguard of the proletariat, the leader of the whole society. All ruling Communist parties had a constitutional monopoly on power. The first rule in George Orwell's *Animal Farm,* "All animals are equal, but some are more equal," precisely describes the situation in the Communist countries: party members were more equal than others. From top to bottom of society, party members were the bosses: there were party cells in each village, in each school, in each factory, in each army unit. These cells made the real decisions about everything—from the "correct party line" concerning some regional conflict at the other side of the world to the handling of young people with unconventional hairdos or a love for Western music. One can visualize the party as a huge pyramid, with directives coming from the top down to the lowest levels.

The party and the state were intertwined, but the party was decisive. In several European countries there were other "shadow" political parties, but they were totally dependent on the Communists and were just "window dressing" in the game of democracy.

Another element in this "let's pretend" game was the elections, an important Communist ritual that was supposed to prove that the ruling parties—which proclaimed themselves to be the parties of the working class—enjoyed the full support of the people. But there was no choice because there was just one candidate for each position. Every citizen was obliged to participate, and the results were always just below 100 percent —99.55 percent or a similar figure, allowing for a few malcontents to disagree with the "party line."

The persons occupying high party and state positions were collectively known as the *nomenclature,* a rather closed group of insiders who

For decades, Communist government bodies simply rubber-stamped the decisions of the party elite. A strong personality cult evolved around the early leaders of the Communist era.

ruled the country. The nomenclature included all top party bosses, government ministers, chairmen of important state agencies, directors of large industrial enterprises and banks, and high army officers. A crucial part of the nomenclature was the secret police. Known as the KGB in the Soviet Union, *Sigurimi* in Albania, *Securitate* in Romania, and *Stasi* in East Germany, the secret police was a powerful force in all of Eastern Europe. There were differences in the secret police between individual countries, ranging from the almost total grip on society by the Albanian and Romanian varieties, to the somewhat more liberal Hungarian and Polish versions. Tens of thousands of people helped the police as informers.

The Ruling Ideology of Marxism-Leninism.   In its most simplistic form, Marxism-Leninism was a set of formulas and pronouncements that, by being endlessly repeated, were at least partially accepted by a great number of people. "All history until the advent of socialism was marked by class struggle between the oppressors and the oppressed" was one such formula; others ranged from a condemnation of profit-making as antisocial, to the notion that the party is the protector of the working people, and to the adulation of the Soviet Union as the "cradle of socialism." Another theme endlessly repeated concerned the sacrifices undergone by Communists in the struggle against Nazism. From kindergarten to university, students had to take classes in Marxism-Leninism and learn by rote the various dogmas. The enforcement of this systematic brainwashing varied in time and by country: the indoctrination gradually became quite perfunctory in Poland and in Hungary; in the conservative regimes such as Romania or Bulgaria, no one dared to challenge the official preaching ideology; in "normalized" Czechoslovakia, almost everyone paid lip service to it even though no one believed in it.

People living in Communist countries grew used to having decisions made for them by the government. Education, child care (below), and medical care, though free, did not meet Western standards.

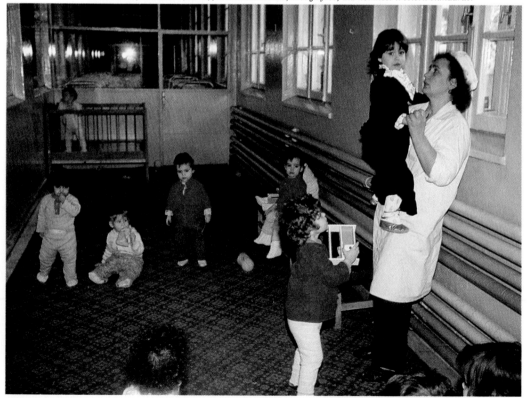

Communist countries tended to concentrate their resources on heavy industry. Much of this industry now needs extensive revamping to make quality products for a world marketplace.

In the early period of the Communist era, Marxism-Leninism was professed with a religious fervor by many people. A believing Communist often resembled a member of a dogmatic sect with whom you can talk for hours, and who always counters your objections with a ready argument. But over the years, Marxism-Leninism turned into a hollow incantation of phrases. It is very probable that when Romania's leader, Nicolae Ceauşescu, talked about the "radiant summits of Communism" in December 1987, most of the undernourished, freezing Romanian population did not believe him.

Command Economy. Command economy (also called a centrally planned economy or a Marxist economy) was for decades hailed as the true "scientific" way to direct the economic life of a society. It has by now become obvious to everyone that command economy brought economic ruin to all countries where it had been implemented. It had several basic characteristics:

● *Central Planning:* Economic decisions were made by huge bureaucracies. Individual entrepreneurship, initiative, and industriousness were not only unwelcome, but were often punished by demotion, harassment, or other means.

● *Price Controls:* All prices were set by the state agencies and often remained unchanged for years.

● *State as the Major Employer:* The state sector was by far the largest one, and so most of the population worked for the state. There was no unemployment, and to fire a person for incompetence was so difficult that it almost never happened (people could easily be fired for political reasons, however). Because salaries were uniformly low, there was no incentive to work hard, and a typical person, whether blue or white collar, worked as little as possible.

- *Emphasis on Heavy Industry:* This went back to Stalin and to his preference for huge industrial complexes. One Romanian superfactory used more electricity than all the private homes throughout the country, for instance. Most of these mammoth enterprises were quite inefficient.
- *Neglect of Services and Chronic Shortages:* This was the other side of the coin of heavy industrialization. Not only were there not enough stores, repair shops, restaurants, and other services, but those that existed were poorly supplied. The shortages varied country by country, from the lack of basic foodstuffs in Romania to occasional shortages of particular items in Czechoslovakia or Hungary.
- *Undeveloped Banking System:* Virtually everything was paid for in cash: salaries, wages, and all purchases. When you paid your rent and utilities, you had to go to a post office and send a money order. Merchandise could not be bought on installment plans, and there were no credit cards.
- *"Shadow Economy" and Black Market* were necessary complements to the malfunctioning official economic system. Almost everyone stole from the state, and some items, such as building materials (cement, bricks, wood) were often stolen on a grand scale. Because it was so hard to get goods and services, there was a widespread "barter economy" and a network of "connections": someone fixed your broken TV set, and you in return supplied him or her with black-market hard currency; or another person got you a high-quality cut of beef, and you repaid with a bottle of Western perfume.

Daily Life in Communist Societies

After the initial times of terror, Communist countries usually settled into periods of less brutal oppression. Most people had several basic certainties. They knew that unless they provoked the authorities with some political protest or even indiscretion, they would never lose their jobs. They knew that the basic foodstuffs would cost the same in years to come. They knew that they would get free education and free medical care, even if very often of substandard quality. Finally, they could count on retirement pensions at a relatively early age, most often at the age of 55 for women and 60 for men.

The other certainties were the daily, constant frustrations. Just to provide for basic needs like food and clothing required enormous energy: standing in lines every day; going from store to store in search of scarce items and arguing with grumpy salespeople; pushing in overcrowded streetcars or buses; on the streets, trying not to fall into gaping excavations that stayed unfinished for months. And when you got home, you found out that the water was out, or the electricity had been shut off, or your refrigerator had stopped working. To get a plumber or repairman for your appliances could take weeks unless you had the right "connections."

At work, people were generally overburdened with dozens of forms and regulations. Unreliability and inefficiency were pervasive: nonworking telephones, constant delays in deliveries, nonsensical orders from above. At the same time, it was considered perfectly normal to go shopping during working hours or to the hairdresser—and to steal. "Whoever does not steal from the state, steals from his family" was a fitting expression of the attitude of many people toward "state property." Ironically, some passages in Marx's early writing dealing with working conditions in the glorious future of Communism seem to describe the current practices in developed countries: concern for safety, clean and well-lighted working places, efforts to make the work interesting and creative for each individual. In countries ruled by the "vanguard of the working class," however, the workplaces were more often than not dirty, uncomfortable, unpleasant, and unsafe.

Another characteristic feature of Communist societies was the quantity of prohibitions and restrictions that you had to deal with all the time. "In the West, anything that is not expressly forbidden is permitted; while under Communism, anything that is not explicitly permitted is forbidden," said one popular joke. In the U.S.S.R., you not only could not freely travel abroad but you had to have an internal passport to travel within the country. If you wanted to move or change jobs, you had to obtain multiple permissions. If you wanted to remodel your apartment, to install a gas heating system, to get a fishing license, or to apply to a university, you had to get approval stamps from countless agencies. If you felt sick with a flu or a cold, you could not stay home for a day or two: you had to go to your assigned doctor, wait there sometimes for hours, and then get his or her permission not to go to work. Travel was another problem, especially for the travel-eager Central Europeans. They could travel within Eastern Europe, but to get to the West was much more complicated, particularly for East Germans, who especially resented the restrictions. In the Balkan Communist countries, with the exception of Yugoslavia, travel to the West was not permitted at all.

To add insult to injury, the Communist mass media continued to extol the virtues of socialism and to condemn the evils of the West. Communist newspapers were full of long articles praising various accomplishments of socialism, reprints of endless boring speeches by Communist dignitaries, Central Committee resolutions, or diatribes against "antisocialist forces," "imperialist powers," or "hostile military-industrial circles." The favorite approach was not outright lying, but distortion of truth, by quoting a person out of context, by pointing only to negative features and never mentioning the positive ones, by omitting the crucial facts and stressing some secondary circumstance.

Last but not least, there was the continual, ever-present fear. Except in the most oppressive periods, it was not a fear for your life, but rather a fear of losing your job, of having your children barred from higher education, of being denied permission to travel. It was a state of being afraid to speak up, of always lowering your voice when talking about politics in public places, of feeling your stomach tighten whenever you had any dealings with a policeman, of avoiding any political talk when speaking on the phone, and never writing anything "dangerous" in letters. In fact, only some phones were bugged, but you never knew whether your phone was among them; only some letters were opened, but you never knew if yours might be among them. The powers that be were simply referred to as "they," and, in Romania, the most frightening word was a simple "she," meaning Elena Ceauşescu, the country's notorious first lady.

How did people cope with all these indignities? One important haven was culture, which, although restricted and under political pressure from the authorities, often provided the only refuge and sense of normality. Most Eastern Europeans are avid book readers, and, until the upheaval in 1989, books were a precious commodity; when a novel by a popular Western author was to come out, people would often stand in long lines to get it, and many books would be sold out completely within a few hours. Public readings of poetry were the Russian specialty. Western movies usually came with a great delay, sometimes 5 to 10 years after they were made, but for that reason alone, they were greatly anticipated. Theaters were generally somewhat less subject to censorship than were movies and, in various periods, political cabarets flourished—in Czechoslovakia in the mid-1960s, in Poland during the 1970s and 1980s, in East Germany in the 1980s. Even classical pieces were sometimes understood by audiences as having poignant messages for the present: because so much was forbidden, it was often sufficient to make a simple gesture, to say a few well-coined words, and the audience understood and became suddenly united as if sharing a secret.

Another important facet of life under Communism was tuning in to foreign broadcasts. Almost all East Germans could get West German programs on their TV sets, and this daily contrast between a Communist and a Western society belied all the official statements about the glories of socialism. Two radio stations that broadcast in all Eastern European languages, Radio Free Europe and Radio Liberty, also played a crucial role in the unraveling of Communist regimes, particularly during the autumn of 1989.

In the Central European countries, political humor was an important means by which to keep one's sanity and mental balance. Political jokes, often quite mordant and brutal, lightened up the daily grayness and made it easier to bear the constant flow of irritations. In the more oppressive periods, it could be dangerous to tell a political joke, but even in more lenient times, you had to be careful in front of whom you spoke. The jokes made fun of inept functionaries ("Who is the most sincere politician in the world? Miloš Jakeš, [party chief in Czechoslovakia], because he looks like an idiot, speaks like an idiot, and is an idiot."), of dumb policemen, of the Soviet Union, of all the official pretensions and lies ("What is socialism? A tortuous way from capitalism to capitalism."). When family and friends met, the newest political jokes were always a welcome part of the conversation.

And finally, there was religion. The new "scientific" ideology of Marxism-Leninism was supposed to replace the old superstitious religious teachings that, according to the official atheist propaganda, had only served the oppressors in their exploitation of the masses. Karl Marx's slogan "religion is the opium of the people" was repeated millions of times after 1917 in the U.S.S.R. and later in Eastern Europe as well. And yet, despite decades of pressure and harassment and persecution, religion has survived. There were great differences between individual countries, ranging from the fiercely antireligious Albania, which closed down all places of worship in 1967, to Poland, a devoutly Catholic country where the church played a large role in social and, in recent decades, political life as well. Soviet Jews, who were in the forefront of the dissident movement, combined their religious yearnings with political activism. The Protestant church in East Germany was involved in the unofficial peace movement during the 1980s, and an underground church existed in Czechoslovakia.

Reform-minded demonstrators always risked being arrested by uniformed or undercover police.

The Fall of Communism

In the spring of 1989, very few people sensed an approaching drama in Eastern Europe. Soviet perestroika was in its fourth year, and many observers both inside the U.S.S.R. and in the West felt a cautious optimism that a gradual transformation of the Communist system was indeed possible. In Poland, the banned trade union Solidarity was being readmitted into the official political arena; in Hungary, the disintegration of Communist authority was proceeding calmly, step by step.

On the other hand, East Germany, Czechoslovakia, Romania, Bulgaria, and Albania seemed to be firmly in the grip of Communist conservatives. A few demonstrations in Prague, Czechoslovakia, were briskly and efficiently suppressed. Yugoslavia occasionally appeared in the news as a country with ethnic problems, but generally it seemed that in most of Eastern Europe the near future would not bring any major changes to the long-entrenched regimes.

When Hungary ordered the Hungarian-Austrian border to be opened in early May 1989, it still did not feel like the beginning of the end. In late summer, however, after Poland installed its first non-Communist prime minister and the exodus of East Germans to the west through Hungary picked up speed, the world began to tune in. Thanks to television, it was the first time in history that millions of people in dozens of countries could watch with fascination a massive upheaval that would transform the face of Europe and the world.

The sequence of events is well known: demonstrations in East German cities in the early fall of 1989; the breaching of the Berlin Wall on

November 9; the demise of the Bulgarian Communist leadership; the "Velvet Revolution" in Czechoslovakia; and the bloody conflict in Romania, which culminated in the trial and execution of the Ceauşescus. At the beginning of 1990, there were only two remaining Communist regimes in Eastern Europe: Yugoslavia and Albania. They both began to unravel in January: in the former country, when the Slovenian delegation quit the party Congress; in the latter, when the first anti-Stalinist demonstrations took place in the city of Shkodër.

During 1990, the two Germanys embarked on the road to unification; in October, they became one country. Poland, Czechoslovakia, Hungary, Romania, and Bulgaria were in ferment, grappling with political, economic, and social turmoil. In Yugoslavia, the two northern republics, Slovenia and Croatia, began to press for more autonomy within the federation, but their demands met with strong opposition from the Serbian leader Slobodan Milosević, a hard-line Communist turned fierce nationalist. To the south, the Albanian reform Communists, in a vain effort to have their cake and eat it too, were frantically introducing reforms to placate a restive population. Meanwhile, economic hardships and disintegration of political authority continued to undermine the position of Mikhail Gorbachev in the Soviet Union. Calls for independence and sovereignty became more strident, not only from the Baltic states, but from other Soviet republics as well.

The following year, 1991, began with a violent crackdown in the Baltics, and continued with the first multi-party elections in Albania in March. In April, Gorbachev and leaders of nine Soviet republics agreed to prepare a new Union treaty, giving all the Soviet republics much greater autonomy. In June, Boris Yeltsin became the first-ever popularly elected leader of Russia. Back in Europe, bloody clashes between Croats and Serbs escalated after Croatia and Slovenia declared independence in late June.

On August 19, 1991, the whole world held its breath when the news about Gorbachev's deposition broke out. Within 24 hours, however, the initial fear began to dissipate as the plotters turned out to be a rather pathetic group of bunglers. The most exhilarating picture of those days was the indomitable Boris Yeltsin on the steps of the Moscow "White House," shielded by his lieutenants with a makeshift board. The saddest moment was the speech by a shaky Gorbachev, after his release from the house arrest, in which he promised to fight for the renewal of the Communist party. The man who had been bold and visionary enough to attempt to free the Soviet Union from its past was suddenly overtaken by history.

The final dismemberment of the Communist superpower, during the following four months, was surprisingly orderly and peaceful, starting with Moscow's acknowledgement of the independence of the Baltic states in September and ending with the official demise of the Soviet Union in late December. In contrast, the dismemberment of Yugoslavia turned bloodier every day: fighting in Croatia continued until early January 1992.

The highlights of the year 1992 include a ferocious war in another former Yugoslav republic, Bosnia-Herzegovina, and bloody conflicts in several parts of the former Soviet Union. The fighting between Armenia and Azerbaijan over the enclave of Nagorny Karabakh, which had begun

The botched coup by Soviet hardliners in August 1991 hastened the collapse of the Soviet Union. A shaken Mikhail Gorbachev (right, returning to Moscow after the coup) resigned on December 25, 1991, and the Soviet Union passed into history.

in 1988, long before the Soviet collapse, intensified throughout 1992 and into 1993. Other clashes in the Caucasus involved small ethnic groups along the border between Russia and Georgia. Still more ethnic violence took place in Moldova, pitting the Slavic minority against the Romanian Moldovans. The war in Tajikistan, on the other hand, was more a struggle between the hard-line Communist "old guard" and new democratic forces. In contrast to all this fighting, the splitting of Czechoslovakia into two independent countries, the Czech and Slovak republics, initiated in mid-1992 and completed on January 1, 1993, proceeded without a single shot being fired.

It will take some time before all the dust settles after the upheaval of recent years, and only with a longer perspective will it be possible to make more reasoned judgments about the rise and fall of Communism. But even now, when it is still an ongoing process, it is possible to list several reasons why this upheaval happened, and why it occurred with such apparent suddenness.

If you had peered under the calm surface of these regimes, you could have seen that their societies were sick and getting sicker every day. The economic system did not work: it was inefficient and often failed to provide even the basic necessities. The environment was abused, with dirty rivers, polluted air, and dying forests. The political system was stifling; most of the popular support for the Communist regimes had already evaporated. Cynicism, feelings of hopelessness, and desperation were pervasive, and corruption was everywhere. Since the authorities tried to suppress any innovation or new idea, thousands of young, talented people tried to leave the Communist countries, often risking their lives. Ugly shabbiness marked the daily life of the people, from the industrial cities in East Germany to cotton plantations in Uzbekistan. The glorious dream proved to be a failure.

The demise of the Communist regimes came as a surprise to many people but it was not really a surprising development. With hindsight it seems even more surprising that it lasted so long.

LIFE AFTER COMMUNISM: A year-by-year overview

THE SOVIET UNION	ALBANIA	BULGARIA	CZECHOSLOVAKIA	EAST GERMANY

1944-1950

The wartime alliance between the U.S.S.R. and England, France, and the **U.S.** sours and turns into the **Cold War**.

The U.S.S.R. helps establish Communist regimes in **Eastern Europe**.

In January 1949, the Council for Mutual Economic Assistance (**COMECON**) is set up.

In November 1944, a Communist government under Enver Hoxha is set up.

In 1946, Albania becomes a People's Republic.

In 1948, Albania severs relations with **Yugoslavia**.

In September 1944, Soviet troops enter the country, and the Communist Party rises to power.

In October 1946, a People's Republic of Bulgaria is proclaimed.

In May 1945, Soviet troops enter the country.

In free elections in May 1946, the Communists emerge as the strongest party, with 38% of the vote.

In February 1948, Communists take power in a bloodless coup.

In June 1948, Czechoslovakia is proclaimed a People's Democracy.

In May 1945, **Germany** is divided into four zones; eastern Germany comes under the Soviet rule. Berlin is divided into four sectors.

In October 1949, the German Democratic Republic is founded.

In 1950, Walter Ulbricht becomes the general secretary of the Communist Party (called German Socialist Unity Party).

1953

Stalin dies in March.

A workers' uprising in June is suppressed by the Soviet armed forces.

1955

Warsaw Pact is established in May.

▲ *Agreements made at the Yalta Conference in 1945 helped shape European history for decades to come.*

1956

In February, **Khrushchev** denounces **Stalin's** crimes in a secret speech at a party congress and initiates the **de-Stalinization** process.

In 1956, an anti-Communist ▶ *uprising in Hungary was brutally suppressed by Soviet troops.*

1958

1960

A split between the U.S.S.R. and China becomes public; for the next three decades, the two countries will go through long periods of tension and even open hostilities.

◀ *During his years as Soviet premier, Nikita Khrushchev tried to reform many aspects of the Communist system. He was ousted from power in 1964.*

HUNGARY	POLAND	ROMANIA	YUGOSLAVIA	THE WEST AND OTHER COUNTRIES	
In October 1944, Soviet troops enter the country. During 1948-49, the Hungarian Workers' Party (Communists) gradually assumes power by breaking up other parties. In August 1949, Hungary is proclaimed a People's Democracy.	In July 1944, Soviet troops enter the country. In January 1947, a bloc of four parties dominated by the Communists wins elections. Subsequently, the Communists (known as the Polish United Workers' Party) assume full power.	In August 1944, Soviet troops enter the country. In March 1945, a Communist-led government is set up. A People's Republic is proclaimed in December 1947.	Led by **Josip Broz Tito**, a war hero, the Yugoslav Communists form a government in March 1945. In 1948, **Tito** refuses to acknowledge **Stalin**'s supremacy, and the Soviet Union breaks relations with Yugoslavia. From then on, **Tito** pursues an "independent road toward **socialism**."	**Cold War** starts during 1945-48. In March 1946, Sir Winston Churchill coins the expression **Iron Curtain**. In April 1949, **NATO** is established. During 1948-49, the **U.S.** and other Allies supply blockaded West Berlin in the Berlin Airlift.	1944-1950
			Diplomatic relations between the **U.S.S.R.** and Yugoslavia are restored.	The Korean War, during 1950-1953, claims 54,246 **U.S.** casualties.	1953
					1955
In October, Budapest rises in an anti-Communist revolt, but the uprising is brutally suppressed by the Soviet armed forces. **János Kádár**, with Soviet help, becomes the new leader of the country. Until 1989, the uprising would be officially labeled as **counterrevolution**.	In June, workers riot in Poznań, and Władysław Gomułka becomes the first secretary of the Communist Party; subsequently he introduces some liberal reforms and improves relations with the church.		Yugoslavia denounces the suppression of the Hungarian uprising.		1956
In June, Imre Nagy, prime minister during the 1956 uprising, is hanged for treason.					1958
				After one year in power, Fidel Castro has transformed **Cuba** into a strident Communist state.	1960

Fidel Castro's revolution transformed ▶ Cuba into the first Communist country in the Western Hemisphere.

1961

The U.S.S.R. installs nuclear missiles in **Cuba**, but under **U.S.** pressure the missiles are dismantled in October, in the Cuban Missile Crisis.

Albania breaks off relations with the **Soviet Union**, accusing **Khrushchev** of **revisionism**.

In August, the East German army erects the **Berlin Wall** and seals off West Berlin.

1963

In 1961, East Germany built the Berlin Wall ▶ around West Berlin. The wall stood for 28 years as a dramatic symbol of the Cold War.

1964

In October, **Khrushchev** is ousted and replaced by **Brezhnev**.

1965

The New Economic Model, giving individual enterprises more autonomy, is adopted.

1967

Following the Six-Day War, the U.S.S.R. condemns Israel and breaks off diplomatic relations.

The government closes all places of worship and declares the country an atheist state.

At a writers' congress in June, an open criticism of party leadership is voiced.

1968

In August, the U.S.S.R. leads a **Warsaw Pact** invasion of **Czechoslovakia** to crush the **Prague Spring**.

In September, the so-called **Brezhnev Doctrine** is formulated, justifying the right of the U.S.S.R. to intervene militarily in any Soviet-bloc country "in defense of **socialism**."

Albania formally withdraws from the **COMECON** and the **Warsaw Pact**.

In January, **Alexander Dubček** becomes the first secretary of the party and announces his goal of "**socialism** with a human face." The ensuing period of reform becomes known as the **Prague Spring**; it is crushed in August, when about 500,000 **Warsaw Pact** troops invade the country.

1969

In April, **Dubček** is replaced by Gustáv Husák.

1970

Czechoslovakia enters the period of "normalization," which freezes the country for two decades.

Willi Stoph, the chairman of the State Council, visits West Germany. It is the highest official visit since the founding of East Germany.

▲
The 1968 "Prague Spring" liberalization movement in Czechoslovakia flourished briefly before being crushed by Warsaw Pact troops.

HUNGARY	POLAND	ROMANIA	YUGOSLAVIA	THE WEST AND OTHER COUNTRIES	
Kádár puts forward the slogan, "Whoever is not against us is with us," in a first effort to heal the division of the country following the 1956 uprising.			The nonaligned movement of Third-World countries is formally inaugurated in Belgrade.	**U.S.** military involvement in **Vietnam** starts. In April, **U.S.**-trained Cuban exiles attempt to overthrow Castro's regime in the Bay of Pigs invasion.	1961
				In November, President John F. Kennedy is assassinated.	1963
In April, **Khrushchev** labels the Hungarian system "goulash **Communism**."			◄ *In 1963, President Kennedy signed a treaty that banned all but underground nuclear-weapon tests.*		1964
		In June, **Nicolae Ceauşescu** becomes the first secretary of the Communist Party.	Yugoslavia introduces far-reaching economic reforms, providing for workers' self-management.		1965
		Romania is the only Soviet-bloc country that does not break relations with Israel.		Israel is the winner in the Six-Day War with Arab states.	1967
The New Economic Mechanism is introduced in January, providing for economic decentralization.	In the spring, students in major cities riot, protesting censorship and political repression. The government subsequently embarks on an anti-Semitic campaign, and many Jews are forced to leave the country.	Romania supports the **Prague Spring** and denounces the August invasion of **Czechoslovakia** by **Warsaw Pact** forces.	Yugoslavia supports the **Prague Spring** and denounces the invasion of **Czechoslovakia** by **Warsaw Pact** forces.	In the spring, students riot in Paris against the Gaullist regime. In April, Martin Luther King, Jr., is assassinated; in June, Senator Robert Kennedy is shot and fatally wounded.	1968
				In July, the first **U.S.** astronauts land on the moon.	1969
	In December, a shipyard workers' protest is brutally suppressed, and at least 44 people are killed. Gomułka is replaced by Edward Gierek.			West German Chancellor **Willy Brandt** initiates his "Eastern policy" of improved relations with the Communist countries by visiting **East Germany**.	1970

19

1972

The U.S.S.R. and the **U.S.** conclude the SALT I treaty, limiting the number of offensive nuclear missiles.

East and West Germany conclude a treaty on economic, political, and cultural cooperation. The treaty also affirms the inviolability of their borders.

1973

Alexander Solzhenitsyn publishes his *Gulag Archipelago*, denouncing the Soviet penal system. Early the next year, he is expelled from the U.S.S.R.

▲

In 1972, U.S. President Nixon and Soviet leader Brezhnev signed the SALT I agreements, which limited the antiballistic missile systems of both countries.

1975

1977

Albania breaks off relations with **China**, accusing it of "social imperialist" policies.

In January, a human-rights manifesto called **Charter 77** is made public, and the authorities respond with a crackdown.

1978

A short-lived cultural "thaw" is initiated by **Zhivkov's** daughter, Lyudmila Zhivkova.

1979

In late December, the U.S.S.R. intervenes in **Afghanistan**.

The New Economic Mechanism, providing for decentralization of the economic policy-making in agriculture, is introduced.

1980

◄ *The U.S. Senate refused to ratify the SALT II agreements, signed by Soviet leader Brezhnev and U.S. President Carter in 1979, when the U.S.S.R. invaded Afghanistan.*

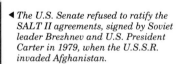

1981

Lyudmila Zhivkova dies, and the "thaw" initiated by her comes to an end.

West German Chancellor Helmut Schmidt visits East Germany.

HUNGARY	POLAND	ROMANIA	YUGOSLAVIA	THE WEST AND OTHER COUNTRIES	

Nicolae Ceaușescu ruled Romania for 25 years, beginning in 1964. His wife, Elena, was considered the second most powerful person in the country.

				In February, **U.S.** President Nixon visits **China**. In May, President Nixon visits Moscow; it is the first visit to the **U.S.S.R.** by a **U.S.** president.	1972
				In January, **Vietnam** peace pacts are signed in Paris. In September, the Marxist government of Chile is overthrown.	1973
			President Tito (below right, with an official visitor from China) made Yugoslavia into a relatively liberal socialist country. ▼	In August, 35 countries sign the **Helsinki Accords**, pledging inviolability of borders and respect for human rights.	1975
		About 35,000 miners in the Jiu Valley strike because of economic grievances.			1977
Hungary establishes diplomatic relations with the Vatican.	In October, the archbishop of Cracow, Karol Cardinal Wojtyła, becomes Pope **John Paul II**.				1978
	In June, **John Paul II** visits Poland.	The government introduces the New Economic-Financial Mechanism, providing for workers' self-management.		In January, the **U.S.** and **China** establish diplomatic relations.	1979
	Workers begin to strike, and, in August, form an independent labor union, **Solidarity**. The strikers are led by **Lech Wałęsa**.			◄ *In 1981, Poland's Solidarity movement became the first independent trade union to be recognized in the Communist bloc.*	1980
	In February, General **Wojciech Jaruzelski** becomes prime minister. Dec. 13, **Jaruzelski** declares martial law, arrests the leadership of **Solidarity**, and suspends the union.			In January, **Ronald Reagan** becomes president of the **U.S.** In March, Pope **John Paul II** barely escapes an assassination attempt.	1981

21

	THE SOVIET UNION	ALBANIA	BULGARIA	CZECHOSLOVAKIA	EAST GERMANY
1982	**Brezhnev** dies in October and is succeeded by Yuri Andropov.		The New Economic Mechanism, providing for decentralization of the economic policy-making in industry, trade, and transport, is introduced.		
1983			Italian investigators charge that Bulgarian agents were involved in the attempted assassination of Pope **John Paul II** in March 1981.	▲ *The Soviet invasion of Afghanistan turned into a 10-year guerrilla war against well-armed rebels.*	
1984	Andropov dies in February and is replaced by Konstantin Chernenko.		Between December 1984 and March 1985, the government forces up to 1 million ethnic Turks (Muslims) to adopt Bulgarian and Christian names.		During 1984, 34,982 East German citizens are permitted to emigrate legally to West Germany.
1985	Chernenko dies on March 10 and, the same day, **Mikhail Gorbachev** becomes the new party secretary. He immediately begins his anticorruption and antialcoholism campaign.	In April, Enver Hoxha dies and is succeeded by **Ramiz Alia**.	*The U.S.S.R. was widely ▶ criticized for its secrecy following the nuclear accident at Chernobyl.*		
1986	In April, a nuclear accident happens at Chernobyl. **Gorbachev** sets up two goals: **perestroika** (economic restructuring) and **glasnost** (political and social opening).		In March, the Italian court rules that there is insufficient evidence to prove Bulgarian complicity in the attempted assassination of Pope **John Paul II**.		In May, East and West Germany sign their first cultural and educational agreement.
Jan.-June 1987	On Jan. 28, the Communist Party Central Committee endorses **Gorbachev**'s proposals for economic and social reforms.	During the year, Albania establishes diplomatic relations with West Germany (in October), Jordan, Canada, Uruguay, and Bolivia.			On April 23, **Honecker** indicates that East Germany would not follow the Soviet model of **glasnost** and **perestroika**.

In October, **Solidarity** is effectively dissolved.

In November, **Lech Wałęsa** is released after 11 months of internment.

On July 22, martial law is lifted.

In October, **Lech Wałęsa** gets the Nobel Peace Prize.

▲ *In 1983, a May Day demonstration by Solidarity supporters in Gdańsk, Poland, was violently dispersed by police.*

In July, the government announces a sweeping amnesty.

In October, a popular priest, Jerzy Popiełuszko, is murdered by two secret agents.

In February, four security officers are convicted and sentenced to long prison terms for the murder of Father Popiełuszko.

In November, **Gorbachev** meets with President **Reagan** in Geneva.

In September, the government announces a sweeping amnesty, which affects 71,500 people, including 1,070 political offenders.

▲ *Father Popiełuszko, a popular priest murdered by Polish security police, quickly became a hero of the anti-Communist movement.*

In December, Presidents **Gorbachev** and **Reagan** meet in Reykjavik, Iceland.

John Paul II visits Poland during June 8-14, and openly advocates political pluralism and human rights.

On May 25-27, **Gorbachev** visits Romania, but his speech on **glasnost** and **perestroika** is received without enthusiasm.

In early 1987, Yugoslav media report that there are about 500 political prisoners in the country, mostly ethnic Albanians.

In June, during his visit to West Berlin, President **Reagan** calls on **Mikhail Gorbachev** to tear down the **Berlin Wall**.

◀ *The Catholic Church, led by John Paul II, the first Polish pope ever, helped inspire the Polish people to challenge Communist rule.*

1982

1983

1984

1985

1986

Jan.–June 1987

23

July–Dec. 1987

On Nov. 2, **Gorbachev** says that **Stalin** had committed enormous crimes.

On Nov. 11, the outspoken **Boris Yeltsin** is dismissed from the Moscow municipal party committee, after being accused by **Gorbachev** of excessive personal ambition and vanity.

In August, an article in the Writers' Union paper *Drita* accuses the Soviet Union of heading toward "barefaced capitalism."

Augustin Navrátil writes a 31-point petition calling for religious freedom. By September 1988, the petition gathers over 500,000 signatures.

On December 17, Gustáv Husák is replaced by Miloš Jakeš as party secretary, but retains his largely ceremonial post of president. In his speech, Jakeš verbally endorses **perestroika**.

During September 7-11, **Erich Honecker** visits West Germany; it is the first visit ever to West Germany by an East German head of state. **Honecker** pays a visit to his own birthplace in Neunkirchen, and also meets with his sister.

Jan.–Feb. 1988

On Feb. 8, **Gorbachev** announces that the pullout of Soviet troops from **Afghanistan** will begin on May 15, 1988, and will be completed within 10 months.

On Feb. 11, thousands of protesters in the **Nagorny-Karabakh** Region in **Azerbaijan** demand reunification with **Armenia**. On Feb. 28, at least 23 Armenians are killed in Sumgait.

Albania raises its diplomatic relations with **Bulgaria** to ambassadorial level.

On Feb. 23-26, Albania participates in the conference of foreign ministers of six Balkan countries in Belgrade. It is an important step out of Albania's diplomatic isolation.

On Jan. 28-29, the Bulgarian Communist Party holds a special party conference to discuss **perestroika**.

On Feb. 29, elections for municipal and regional councils take place; it is the first time that the ballot includes more than one candidate. Over a quarter of the elected deputies have been independent candidates, not affiliated with the Communist Party.

On Jan. 11, Miloš Jakeš visits Moscow for talks with **Gorbachev**. The latter says after the meeting that "innovative policies" are needed in Europe.

On Jan. 26-28, West German Chancellor **Helmut Kohl** visits Czechoslovakia; in addition to meeting with the officials, **Kohl** also meets with representatives of **Charter 77**.

On Jan. 7, **Erich Honecker** begins a three-day visit to France. President Mitterrand and Premier Chirac criticize East German human-rights practices and the existence of the **Berlin Wall**.

On Jan. 17, about 120 persons are arrested during a **dissident** demonstration in East Berlin.

March–April 1988

On March 13, *Sovietskaya Rossiya* newspaper publishes a letter by Mrs. Nina Andreyevna, attacking **glasnost** and **perestroika**. This conservative manifesto is said to be personally endorsed by **Ligachev**.

In March, several articles tentatively praise certain aspects of the Soviet **glasnost**. At the same time, however, the media criticize as "absurd" the current Soviet condemnations of **Stalin**.

On March 5-6, about 80 persons are arrested during human-rights manifestations in East Berlin and other cities.

May 1988

On May 7-9, a political opposition group known as the Democratic Union is founded in Moscow.

In 1988, many Soviet ▶ people turned out for celebrations marking the one-thousandth anniversary of the introduction of Christianity into Russia.

| | On Nov. 29, in two related referenda, Polish voters do not endorse political and economic reforms proposed by the government. These are the first referenda ever to take place in a Communist country. | In November and December, antigovernment demonstrations take place in Braşov and several other places. The demonstrators protest against food shortages and restrictions on gas and electricity.

On December 14, **Ceauşescu** says at the extraordinary party conference that Romania does not need any changes because it is on a path toward the "radiant summits of **communism**." | Tensions in the province of **Kosovo**, whose population is predominantly Albanian, increase, and, in October, emergency security measures are adopted. | A summit meeting between Presidents **Reagan** and **Gorbachev** takes place in Washington on December 7-10. The two leaders sign the Intermediate-Range Nuclear Forces Treaty and hail the meeting as a success. |

| | On Feb. 1, prices of goods and services rise an average of 27%, including 40% increases for basic food, 100% for gas and electricity, and 200% for coal. Protest demonstrations take place in Warsaw and Gdańsk. | | On Feb. 24-26, Belgrade hosts a meeting of foreign ministers from **Albania**, **Bulgaria**, Greece, **Romania**, Turkey, and Yugoslavia. It is the first such regional meeting since the early 1930s. | |

| | On April 25, price increases spark a two-week wave of strikes, the gravest labor unrest since the imposition of martial law in December 1981. | On Apr. 5, the government announces that it intends to reduce the number of Romanian villages from about 13,000 to some 6,000 to 7,000, and replace them with "agro-industrial centers," in the so-called "systematization plan." | On March 14-18, **Gorbachev** visits Yugoslavia and admits that the rift between the **U.S.S.R.** and Yugoslavia dating from 1948 was the Soviet Union's fault. | |

| On May 14, the first independent trade union (Trade Union of Scientific Workers) is formed.

On May 22, **János Kádár** is replaced by Károly Grósz. | | | | Between May 29 and June 2, President **Ronald Reagan** of the **U.S.** visits the **U.S.S.R.** It is Mr. **Reagan's** first visit to the country that he labeled "an evil empire" just a few years ago. |

June 1988

During June 5-16, celebrations of the 1,000th anniversary of the conversion to Christianity are held in the U.S.S.R.

On June 20, **Estonia** officially recognizes the People's Front of **Estonia**, which becomes the first non-Communist political group to gain official recognition in the U.S.S.R.

◄ *By means of a U.N.-media agreement, the U.S.S.R. be to withdraw its troops fron Afghanistan in 1988. All t₁ troops were home by mid-February 1989.*

Aug.-Sept. 1988

On Aug. 21, the 20th anniversary of the 1968 invasion, about 10,000 people demonstrate in the center of Prague. It is the largest public protest since 1969, but it is broken up by riot police and tear gas.

Oct. 1988

On Oct.1-2, the **Estonian** Popular Front for **Perestroika** holds its inaugural congress.

On Oct. 9, the **Latvian** Popular Front holds its founding congress.

On Oct. 10, Premier Lubomír Štrougal, the main advocate of economic reforms, is forced to resign.

On Oct. 10, about 80 persons are arrested in East Berlin during a demonstration against censorship of church publications.

Nov. 1988

On Nov. 22, eight people are killed and 126 wounded in violence between **Armenians** and **Azerbaijanis**.

Diplomatic relations with **Hungary** are raised to ambassadorial level.

On Nov. 3, 80 leading intellectuals found the Club for Support of **Glasnost** and **Perestroika.**

Dec. 1988

On Dec. 7, an earthquake registering 6.9 on the Richter scale strikes **Armenia**, killing at least 25,000 people.

On Dec. 23, Bulgaria stops jamming Radio Free Europe.

On Dec. 1, **Honecker** criticizes the Soviet media for "attempting to rewrite Soviet history in a bourgeois manner."

◄ *In 1988, a strong earthquake in Armenia caused widespread destruction of property and untold suffering to the people.*

June 1988

Between 30,000 and 50,000 Hungarians demonstrate against the Romanian plan to raze as many as 7,000 ethnic Hungarian villages in **Romania** and replace them with agro-industrial complexes.

Local elections take place on June 19, but only 55% of voters participate, which is the lowest turnout since the beginning of Communist rule. **Solidarity** has called for the boycott of the elections.

Aug.-Sept. 1988

On Aug. 28, Hungarian Premier Grósz meets with the Romanian President **Ceauşescu** in an attempt to resolve disputes between Hungary and **Romania** concerning the Romanian plan to raze ethnic-Hungarian villages. The meeting is unsuccessful.

On Aug. 15, strikes begin in Silesian coal mines and quickly spread to other cities. The strikers demand the legalization of **Solidarity**. On Aug. 31, **Lech Wałęsa** begins discussions with the interior minister, Czesław Kiszczak, and then issues a call to the strikers to return to work.

On Sept. 19, former King Michael of Romania, exiled since 1947, issues a call in Switzerland for a revolt against **Ceauşescu**.

▲
In October 1988, the Polish government announced plans to close the Lenin Shipyard in Gdańsk (above), the birthplace of Solidarity.

Oct. 1988

On Oct. 31, the government announces that it will shut down Gdańsk's Lenin Shipyard, birthplace and stronghold of **Solidarity**.

On Oct. 4-6, **Ceauşescu** visits the **U.S.S.R.** During the visit, **Gorbachev** indirectly criticizes Romanian policy and stresses the need for reform.

Nov. 1988

On Nov. 23, Miklós Németh replaces Communist Party Secretary Grósz as premier. Grósz remains general secretary.

Mrs. Thatcher visits Poland on Nov. 2-4 and urges the government to start a dialogue with **Solidarity**.

Dec. 1988

27

Jan. 1989

On Jan. 5, the Central Committee of the Communist Party calls for the mass rehabilitation of "thousands of victims" of the Stalinist purges from the 1930s to the early 1950s.

On Jan. 12, a special decree of the Presidium of the Supreme Soviet places **Nagorno-Karabakh** in **Azerbaijan** under direct rule from Moscow.

During Jan. 15-20, demonstrations take place in Prague, marking the 20th anniversary of the suicide of Jan Palach. The police break up the demonstrations with truncheons, water cannon, tear gas, and dogs. Among the persons arrested is the **dissident** playwright **Václav Havel**.

On Jan. 15, about 80 people are detained during a silent protest march in Leipzig.

Feb. 1989

By Feb. 15, all Soviet troops have left **Afghanistan**. In the nine-year war, about 15,000 Soviet troops were killed, and over 1 million Afghan combatants and civilians perished.

On Feb. 21, **Václav Havel** is sentenced to nine months in prison for "inciting anti-state and anti-social activities." Several other **dissidents** are tried on similar charges.

March 1989

In the March 26 elections for the Congress of People's Deputies, many Communist Party candidates are defeated by representatives of unofficial groups of independents. **Boris Yeltsin** wins a landslide victory in Moscow.

April 1989

On Apr. 9, a pro-independence demonstration in Tbilisi, **Georgia**, is brutally attacked by troops; 20 people die, either clubbed to death or killed by toxic gas.

On Apr. 20, **Andrei Sakharov** is elected to the Congress of People's Deputies.

◄ *Mikhail Gorbachev's policies of glasnost (openness) and perestroika (restructuring) have sent shock waves through Soviet society. One side effect of his programs has been the virtual elimination of the personality cult surrounding Lenin, whose statue or portrait once seemed to loom everywhere.*

HUNGARY	POLAND	ROMANIA	YUGOSLAVIA	THE WEST AND OTHER COUNTRIES	
On Jan. 11, a new law establishes the right to form new political parties. The official reevaluation of the 1956 uprising starts with the unauthorized statement by a leading reformer, Imre Pószgay, on Jan. 28, that the 1956 revolt was a "popular uprising," not a **counterrevolution**.	On Jan. 18, the plenum of the Central Committee of the Communist Party approves a resolution authorizing negotiations with **Solidarity** and its participation in round-table discussions about Poland's future.		On Jan. 11, an opposition party calling itself the Democratic Alliance is inaugurated in Ljubljana, the capital of **Slovenia**. On Jan. 19, the collective state presidency designates **Ante Marković** the federal prime minister of Yugoslavia.	In January, **George Bush** becomes **U.S.** president.	Jan. 1989
On Feb. 16, the party historical commission publishes a report on the 1956 uprising, which rejects the designation **counterrevolution** and sharply condemns the Stalinist regimes imposed on the countries in **Eastern Europe**. On Feb. 22, the government announces that the anniversary of the 1917 October Revolution in **Russia** will no longer be celebrated in Hungary.	On Feb. 6, round-table talks between the authorities and the banned **Solidarity** union open. The first session, televised nationally, begins with addresses by the Interior Minister Czesław Kiszczak and by the **Solidarity** leader, **Lech Wałęsa**. In the second half of February, anti-Communist and right-wing opposition groups protest against the round-table talks.		On Feb. 2, a new opposition party called the Initiative for a Democratic Yugoslavia is formed in Zagreb, **Croatia**. Strikes by ethnic Albanians in **Kosovo** lead to resignation of the provincial party leadership; this provokes a Serbian backlash, which culminates in a 700,000-strong demonstration of Serbs in Belgrade against the "chauvinism and separatism" of Kosovar Albanians.	Western governments strongly protest against the sentences given to Czechoslovak **dissidents**, specifically to **Václav Havel**.	Feb. 1989
March 15 becomes the newly designated public holiday, commemorating the start of the 1848 Hungarian uprising against Austrian rule.		In early March, six former high officials accuse President **Ceaușescu** in an open letter of violating human rights and ruining the country's economy. The letter is published in the West on March 12-13.	On March 16, **Ante Marković** outlines his government program, which consists of a radical transformation of the Yugoslav economy to a free-market system. In early March, Serbian authorities ban public protests in **Kosovo**.		March 1989
On Apr. 22, the Communist Youth Union votes to dissolve itself. On Apr. 25, the **U.S.S.R.** begins a unilateral withdrawal of troops from **Eastern Europe**, starting with Hungary.	On Apr. 6, round-table talks between the authorities and the outlawed **Solidarity** conclude with the signing of three agreements: on trade union pluralism, political reforms, and economic and social policy. On Apr. 17, **Solidarity** is granted legal status.	On Apr. 12, 1989, the government announces that Romanian foreign debt had been paid back in full.		Student demonstrations in support of democracy start in **China** in mid-April.	April 1989

29

May 1989

On May 13-14, over 400 representatives of the **Estonian** and **Latvian** Popular Fronts and the **Lithuanian** Sajudis meet in Tallinn (Estonia) in the first Baltic Assembly.

On May 25, the Congress elects **Gorbachev** to the new post of chairman of the Supreme Soviet (that is, state president).

On May 31, **Boris Yeltsin** criticizes **Gorbachev** for the failures of **perestroika**, and also attacks the **nomenclature** (party and state bureaucracy).

On May 20-21, protests against "bulgarization" by ethnic Turks in north-eastern Bulgaria turn violent. According to official accounts, seven people die, but the unofficial figure is 30.

On May 1, about 2,000 young people stage a pro-democracy demon-stration, but are dis-persed by the police.

On May 17, **Václav Havel** is released from prison after serving four months of his eight-month sentence. The authorities say that he is released because of "good behavior," but Western criticism is a more likely reason.

June 1989

On June 3-4, and again on June 7-8, a violent ethnic conflict takes place in **Uzbekistan** between Uzbeks and Meshketians. The toll is 99 dead and over 1,000 injured.

On June 16-17, ethnic violence takes place in **Kazakhstan**; the toll is four dead and 53 injured.

During June, over 80,000 ethnic Turks leave Bulgaria for Turkey.

On June 29, a petition called *A Few Sentences* is published. Signed by prominent **dissidents**, but also by many people from other sections of society, including the Communist Party, the petition sets out seven basic demands in order to "fundamentally change the social and political climate."

July 1989

On July 10, strikes begin in the Kuzbass coalfield in western Siberia. Within two weeks the strikes spread to the Donbass region of eastern **Ukraine** and to other mines.

On July 27-28, about 300 radical deputies (including **Boris Yeltsin** and **Andrei Sakharov**) form the "Inter-regional Group" within the Congress of People's Deputies, as an unoffi-cial parliamentary oppo-sition.

By the end of July, over 11,500 people sign *A Few Sentences*.

◄ *Andrei Sakharov, a leading Soviet physicist, emerged as an important dissident in the 1960s. In 1975, Sakharov won the Nobel Peace Prize for his human-rights activities. He spent six years in internal exile for his public opposition to Soviet policies before being released by Mikhail Gorbachev in 1986. In 1989, shortly before his death, Sakharov was elected to the U.S.S.R.'s Congress of People's Deputies.*

On May 2, Hungary begins to dismantle the barbed-wire fence on its border with Austria. This measure reportedly angers the authorities in **Czechoslovakia**, **East Germany**, and **Romania**.

On May 8, **János Kádár** is relieved of his post of party president and of his membership in the central committee.

▲
Hungary's dismantling of the fence on its border with Austria sparked a huge exodus of refugees to the West.

During May 15-18, **Gorbachev** visits **China**, and the state and party relations between **China** and the **U.S.S.R.** are formally normalized, after almost 30 years of tensions and animosity.

On May 17, over 1 million people participate in the largest antigovernment demonstration in Beijing, **China**.

On June 13 and 21, the Communist Party leadership holds televised roundtable talks with representatives of political opposition groups.

On June 16, Imre Nagy, prime minister during the 1956 uprising, is reburied in a state funeral. The ceremony is attended by some 300,000 people.

On June 4 and 18, elections for the new bicameral National Assembly are held, and the **Solidarity**-backed candidates win all except one of the "unreserved" seats.

On June 6, **Jaruzelski** invites **Solidarity** to join the government in a broad coalition. **Solidarity** rejects this offer.

On June 3-4, Chinese troops crack down on pro-democracy demonstrations and kill an estimated 2,000 to 5,000 people.

On June 13, **Gorbachev** and **Kohl** sign a "historic" agreement on human rights and economic cooperation.

On July 6, **János Kádár** dies. On the same day, the Hungarian Supreme Court repeals the treason verdicts that were handed down to Imre Nagy and eight of his associates during the 1956 uprising.

On July 11-12, President **Bush** visits Hungary, the first **U.S.** president to do so.

On July 9-10, President **Bush** visits Poland and meets with both **Jaruzelski** and **Wałęsa**. Poles are disappointed with the offered **U.S.** aid because they have expected a larger amount.

On July 19, **Jaruzelski** is elected to the new post of executive president of **Poland**.

On July 7-8, leaders of the **Warsaw Pact** states meet in Bucharest. Although the final communiqué unanimously endorses the current ideological diversity within the socialist bloc, it is reported that an "unprecedented disunity" reigned behind the scenes.

THE SOVIET UNION	ALBANIA	BULGARIA	CZECHOSLOVAKIA	EAST GERMANY

Aug. 1989

THE SOVIET UNION

On Aug. 23, more than a million people in **Lithuania**, **Latvia**, and **Estonia** form a 360-mile-long human chain to commemorate the 50th anniversary of the Soviet-Nazi pact of 1939, which set the stage for the Soviet annexation of the **Baltic republics**.

BULGARIA

By Aug. 21, the number of ethnic Turks fleeing from Bulgaria to Turkey has reached 310,000, and Turkey closes its borders.

CZECHOSLOVAKIA

On Aug. 21, on the anniversary of the 1968 **Warsaw Pact** invasion, several thousand demonstrators clash with the police, and almost 400 people are arrested.

Sept. 1989

THE SOVIET UNION

On Sept. 8-10, the People's Movement of the **Ukraine** (referred to as Rukh) holds its founding congress.

During September, the **Azerbaijan** Popular Front organizes a blockade of **Armenia**.

On Sept. 19, at a meeting of the Central Committee, **Gorbachev** presents a program on nationalities policy, suggesting a restructuring of the Soviet federal system.

CZECHOSLOVAKIA

About 4,000 East Germans take refuge in the West German embassy in Prague during August and September.

EAST GERMANY

Exodus of East Germans across the newly opened border between **Hungary** and Austria gains momentum, by the end of September, more than 24,000 East Germans have fled.

New Forum, an umbrella organization set up to coordinate informal political groups, applies for official recognition, which is denied.

Demonstrations start to take place regularly in Leipzig and other East German cities.

Oct. 1989

THE SOVIET UNION

On Oct. 9, a new labor law recognizes the right to strike; it is the first such recognition in Soviet history.

Ethnic tensions continue in **Armenia**, **Azerbaijan**, and Ossetia in **Georgia**.

On Oct. 13, **Gorbachev** strongly attacks certain editors and journalists for abusing **glasnost**.

On Oct. 17, the published report by the Amnesty International notes that there has been a "dramatic" improvement in the Soviet human rights situation since 1986.

ALBANIA

On Oct. 14, the Eco-Glasnost, an environmental group, begins collecting signatures on a pro-conservation petition.

On Oct. 18, the Independent Association for the Defense of Human Rights stages its first rally, which is attended by about 160 people.

On Oct. 23-24, the authorities start a clampdown on Eco-Glasnost and other unofficial groups, arresting more than 20 people.

CZECHOSLOVAKIA

On Oct. 28, up to 10,000 demonstrators protest in the center of Prague, and the police detain 355 persons.

By the end of the month, the number of signatures on the petition *A Few Sentences* reaches 35,000.

EAST GERMANY

On Oct. 1, a special train with about 4,000 East German refugees leaves Prague for West Germany.

On Oct. 4-5, another train with 10,000 to 11,000 East Germans leaves Prague for West Germany.

On Oct. 6-7, **Gorbachev** visits East Germany for the celebrations of its 40th anniversary. He reportedly warns **Honecker** that leaders who stay behind "put themselves in danger."

On Oct. 18, **Erich Honecker** resigns for "health reasons" and is replaced by Egon Krenz.

On Oct. 30, the weekly protest in Leipzig is attended by more than 300,000 people.

During August, a series of negotiations between the Communists and **Solidarity** culminates in a complete realignment of Polish politics when, on Aug. 24, the parliament elects as prime minister **Tadeusz Mazowiecki**, a leading **Solidarity** member. It is the formal end of the Communist era in Poland.

◀ *In August 1989, Tadeusz Mazowiecki (center) was elected prime minister of Poland, the first non-Communist to achieve that position in any Warsaw Pact country.*

Roundtable talks between the authorities and opposition groups end in a compromise agreement on Sept. 18. The agreement provides for free elections in 1990.

About 600 East Germans take refuge in the West German embassy in Warsaw during August and September.

On Sept. 12, **Mazowiecki** forms a new coalition government dominated by **Solidarity** members.

On Sept. 27, the parliament in **Slovenia** proclaims the republic an "independent, sovereign, and autonomous state," with a right to secession from the Yugoslav federation.

During Sept. 9-18, **Boris Yeltsin** visits the **U.S.**, on a private lecture tour.

Huge demonstrations became a ▶ *regular feature of Czechoslovakia's "velvet revolution" in late 1989.*

During Oct. 6-10, the Hungarian Socialist Workers' Party (the Communist Party) is fundamentally restructured and renamed the Hungarian Socialist Party. The new party pledges its commitment to multiparty democracy and market economy.

On Oct. 17-20, the parliament approves an amended constitution, describing Hungary as an "independent democratic state."

On Oct. 23, the anniversary of the 1956 uprising, the name of the country is formally changed to the "Republic of Hungary."

On Oct. 10, Poland's first stock exchange opens in Warsaw.

On Oct. 12, the government publishes a plan for a quick establishment of a full-fledged market economy.

On Oct. 26-27, foreign ministers of the **Warsaw Pact** countries meet in Warsaw and reject the so-called **Brezhnev Doctrine**. They announce a new policy of recognizing the absolute right of each state to determine its development, which is being referred to popularly as the **Sinatra Doctrine** (the **Warsaw Pact** countries can "do it their way").

Nov. 1989

On Nov. 4-7, the **Armenian** National Movement holds its founding congress.

On Nov. 17-19, the Supreme Soviet of **Georgia** reaffirms the republic's right to secede from the Soviet Union.

On Nov. 27, the **U.S.S.R.** Supreme Soviet grants the **Baltic republics** full right over their resources and autonomy in financial operations.

On Nov. 28, the Supreme Soviet returns the rule over **Nagorno-Karabakh** to **Azerbaijan**.

On Nov. 15, Albania declares an amnesty, which applies to a limited number of political prisoners.

On Nov. 3, about 4,000 people take part in a pro-democracy demonstration outside the National Assembly. It is the largest unofficial demonstration in Bulgaria since 1947.

On Nov. 10, **Todor Zhivkov** is ousted in a "palace coup" and replaced by Petur Mladenov, the foreign minister. Mladenov promises free elections and stresses the urgency of "turning Bulgaria into a modern democratic and law-governed state."

On Nov. 17, an official rally of over 100,000 supports political reforms.

On Nov. 17, an officially approved student demonstration turns into a violent clash with the police.

On Nov. 20, a "demonstration week" begins, with protest rallies growing in numbers and spreading throughout the country.

On Nov. 27, a two-hour general strike is supported by millions of workers.

On Nov. 29, the article guaranteeing the "leading role of the Communist party" is abolished.

On Nov. 4, over 500,000 demonstrate in East Berlin.

On Nov. 7, the whole Politburo of the Communist Party resigns.

On Nov. 8, the New Forum opposition group is legalized.

On Nov. 9, the **Berlin Wall** is opened and several million East Germans visit West Berlin in the first few days.

On Nov. 17, the new prime minister, Hans Modrow, says that speculation about German reunification is "as unrealistic as it is dangerous."

Dec. 1989

On Dec. 1, **Mikhail Gorbachev** meets with **John Paul II**. It is the first meeting ever between a pope and a Soviet head of state.

On Dec. 7, the **Lithuanian** Supreme Court deletes the article guaranteeing the "leading role" of the Communist Party.

On Dec. 14, **Andrei Sakharov** dies of a heart attack.

On Dec. 19-20, the Communist Party of **Lithuania** declares itself independent of the Communist Party of the Soviet Union.

On Dec. 11, **Zhivkov** is expelled from the Communist Party.

On Dec. 10, a new federal government is formed in which the non-Communists have a majority. The same day, President Husák resigns.

On Dec. 17, the border with Austria is opened.

On Dec. 20, the extraordinary congress of the Communist Party adopts a statement apologizing to the Czechoslovak people for "unjustified reprisals" after 1968.

On Dec. 28, **Alexander Dubček** is elected chairman of the Federal Assembly.

On Dec. 29, **Václav Havel** is elected president of the republic.

On Dec. 1, the parliament abolishes the leading role of the Communist Party.

On Dec. 3, a human chain of up to 2 million people joins hands across East Germany, calling for democratic renewal.

On Dec. 7, round-table talks are held with the opposition, and the participants agree that general elections will be held in May 1990.

On Dec. 16-17, the Communist Party changes its name from the "Socialist Unity Party" to "Socialist Unity Party—Party of Democratic Socialism."

◄ *Millions of East Germans visited West Berlin in the first few days after the Berlin Wall was opened.*

On Nov. 26, a referendum narrowly approves the petition of opposition groups to postpone the election of a president after the legislative elections in March 1990.

On Nov. 20-24, the 14th congress of the Romanian Communist Party is held, and **Ceauşescu** is elected for a further five-year term as the general secretary.

On Nov. 28, West German Chancellor **Helmut Kohl** presents a plan for a German confederation that could eventually lead to reunification.

◄ *Romania's overthrow of the Ceauşescu dictatorship was by far the most violent of the 1989 revolutions in Eastern Europe.*

Nov. 1989

On Dec. 29, the parliament approves a radical economic-reform package, to begin on Jan. 1, 1990.

On Dec. 29-30, the formal name of the country is changed to "Polish Republic" (instead of Polish People's Republic).

On Dec. 16, several hundred people protest a deportation order served on a Protestant pastor, Fr. Lázsló Tökes, in Timişoara. Next day, the protests grow larger, and the police fire on the crowd.

On Dec. 22, **Ceauşescu** and his wife are airlifted from the Central Committee headquarters as demonstrators break into the building. The revolutionaries organize themselves into the National Salvation Front (NSF).

On Dec. 25, **Nicolae** and Elena **Ceauşescu** are tried before a military tribunal; condemned to death; and immediately executed.

By Dec. 25, **Ion Iliescu** is named president by the NSF.

On Dec. 28, the country's name is changed to Romania (replacing the Socialist Republic of Romania).

By December, relations between **Slovenia** and **Serbia** deteriorate considerably, leading to the effective closure of the border between the two republics.

On Dec. 2-3, Presidents **Bush** and **Gorbachev** meet aboard **U.S.** and Soviet warships off the coast of Malta for their first summit.

▲ *U.S. President Bush and Soviet President Gorbachev developed a friendly rapport during their first summit meeting in Malta.*

Dec. 1989

THE SOVIET UNION	ALBANIA	BULGARIA	CZECHOSLOVAKIA	EAST GERMANY

Jan. 1990

THE SOVIET UNION

On Jan. 11, the Supreme Soviet of **Latvia** abolishes the "leading role" of the Communist Party.

On Jan. 11-13, **Mikhail Gorbachev** visits **Lithuania**, on a mission to solve the secessionist crisis.

On Jan. 19, Soviet troops assault the city of Baku, **Azerbaijan**, following the escalation of ethnic violence between **Armenians** and **Azerbaijani** that has erupted early in January.

ALBANIA

On Jan. 1, **Ramiz Alia** says in his New Year's message that the country's enemies are renewing "a campaign of slanders" against Albania. He further states that Albania is a "society of justice" without "social conflicts or national oppression."

According to second-hand testimony, anti-Stalinist demonstrations take place on Jan. 11 and 14 in the city of Shkodër, involving up to 7,000 people.

BULGARIA

On Jan. 1-2, anti-Turkish demonstrations break out in southern Bulgaria.

On Jan. 15, the parliament repeals the article guaranteeing the "leading role" of the Communist Party.

On Feb. 2, the 14th extraordinary congress of the Communist Party states in its manifesto that the party is now committed to "human and democratic **socialism**."

CZECHOSLOVAKIA

On Jan. 2, President **Havel** visits **East** and West **Germany**.

On Jan. 25-26, President **Havel** visits **Poland** and **Hungary**.

EAST GERMANY

Throughout January, roundtable talks with opposition groups continue.

On Jan. 15, thousands of protesters ransack the headquarters of the secret police in Berlin.

On Jan. 28, Prime Minister Hans Modrow announces the formation of a government of national responsibility, which includes eight opposition ministers.

Feb. 1990

THE SOVIET UNION

On Feb. 5-7, the Central Committee backs **Gorbachev**'s new platform that clears the way for a multiparty system in the U.S.S.R.

On Feb. 23, the Supreme Soviet of **Estonia** abolishes the article guaranteeing the "leading role" of the Communist Party.

BULGARIA

On Feb. 8, after the opposition groups refuse to join a new coalition government, the National Assembly approves a government that consists solely of Communist ministers.

On Feb. 25, the opposition alliance called Union of Democratic Forces organizes a rally at which 200,000 participate.

CZECHOSLOVAKIA

On Feb. 1, the secret police is abolished.

During Feb. 17-22, President **Havel** visits Iceland, Canada, and the **U.S.**

On Feb. 26-27, **Havel** visits Moscow and confers with **Gorbachev**. They sign an agreement that all 73,500 Soviet troops stationed in Czechoslovakia will depart by July 1991.

EAST GERMANY

On Feb. 1, upon his return from the **U.S.S.R**, Prime Minister Hans Modrow proposes to create a united, neutral **Germany**.

On Feb. 5, the government of national responsibility is installed, with a majority of non-Communists.

On Feb. 13-14, Hans Modrow visits West Germany.

March 1990

THE SOVIET UNION

On March 11, the Supreme Soviet of **Lithuania** declares the republic independent.

On March 13, the Congress of People's Deputies abolishes the monopoly of the Communist Party.

On March 14, **Mikhail Gorbachev** is elected President of the U.S.S.R.

On March 30, the Supreme Soviet of **Estonia** agrees to set in motion a process of secession from the U.S.S.R.

BULGARIA

On March 5, the National Assembly adopts a bill that allows ethnic Turks to resume their original names that they had been compelled to renounce during the forced assimilation in 1984-85.

On March 6, the National Assembly legalizes strikes for the first time in Bulgarian history.

CZECHOSLOVAKIA

Throughout March, the Federal Assembly is engaged in a "hyphen war"—a prolonged debate about the new name of the country. The Slovaks, inhabitants of **Slovakia** in the eastern part of the country, want the name to be spelled "Czecho-Slovakia," but the Czechs reject this spelling.

EAST GERMANY

On March 18, the first free and secret general elections are held in East Germany. The winning party, the Christian Democratic Union, gets 40.8% of the vote; the Communists get 16.4%.

On Jan. 5, the "Danube-gate" scandal breaks open when it is revealed that the Interior Ministry security police have not stopped covert surveillance of opposition politicians, despite amendments creating a multiparty system.

By 1990, Lithuanians (above) and other residents of the Baltic Republics had become very vocal in their demand for independence from the Soviet Union.

On Jan. 27, the Polish Communist Party (named Polish United Workers' Party) decides to disband itself at its 11th and final congress. The gathering then becomes a founding congress of a new party, the Social Democracy of the Polish Republic.

On Jan. 3, the NSF reverses the former regime's prohibition of foreign borrowing.

On Jan. 12, the NSF outlaws the Communist Party of Romania, but the next day the decision is reversed.

On Jan. 28-29, large demonstrations take place in Bucharest, first by the opponents of the National Salvation Front, and then by supporters.

On Jan. 2, Yugoslavia introduces a new dinar worth 10,000 old dinars, in an effort to bring down inflation, which has reached 1,125% in December.

On Jan. 20-23, the 14th extraordinary congress of the Communist Party (League of Communists of Yugoslavia) takes place, but it ends in disarray after the delegation from **Slovenia** walks out.

At the end of January, violence erupts again in the province of **Kosovo**.

On Feb. 1, the National Salvation Front agrees to share power with representatives of 29 opposition parties.

On Feb. 18, about 3,000 to 8,000 demonstrators demand **Ion Iliescu**'s resignation. Next day, 5,000 to 8,000 miners from the Jiu Valley are brought to Budapest in support of the National Salvation Front.

On Feb. 4, the League of Communists of **Slovenia** renounces its links with the League of Communists of Yugoslavia.

On Feb. 13, the four major World War II Allies—France, the **U.S.S.R.**, England, and the **U.S.**—and the two German states agree on a "two-plus-four" formula for the unification of **Germany**.

On Feb. 25, the opposition candidate wins the presidency in **Nicaragua** against the candidate of the Sandinistas.

On March 10, an agreement is signed with the **U.S.S.R.** providing for the complete withdrawal of all 52,000 Soviet troops from Hungary by July 1991.

On March 25, the first round of general elections takes place.

On March 1, the Timişoara Declaration calls for the banning of ex-Communists from public offices.

On March 20, about 2,000 Romanian nationalists attack a peaceful demonstration by 5,000 ethnic Hungarians in Transylvania.

April 1990

On Apr. 6-7, an extraordinary congress of the **Latvian** Communist Party takes place, and ends in a split into independent and pro-Moscow parties.

On Apr. 18, the U.S.S.R. begins an economic blockade of **Lithuania**.

On Apr. 17, **Ramiz Alia** says at the Central Committee's plenum that Albania is no longer opposed to diplomatic ties with the **U.S.S.R.** and with the **U.S.**

On Apr. 3, Petur Mladenov is elected president of Bulgaria.

On Apr. 3, the Communist Party renames itself the Bulgarian Socialist Party.

On Apr. 9, a meeting of Czechoslovak, Hungarian, and Polish leaders is held in Bratislava, to discuss the "return to Europe" of the three countries.

On Apr. 20, the Federal Assembly adopts the new name of the country: Czech and Slovak Federative Republic.

On Apr. 12, a new "grand coalition" government led by the Christian Democratic Union is sworn in.

May 1990

On May 1, following the May Day parade, about 40,000 people from opposition groups denounce Communist rule and President **Gorbachev**.

On May 4, the Supreme Soviet in **Latvia** proclaims **Latvia's** independence from the U.S.S.R.

On May 8, the Supreme Soviet in **Estonia** proclaims **Estonia** independent.

On May 29, **Boris Yeltsin** is elected president of **Russia**.

On May 7-8, the People's Assembly approves judicial and economic reforms and lifts the ban on religious propaganda. According to unofficial reports, there have been demonstrations in several Albanian towns in the previous months.

On May 18, a treaty on "the creation of a monetary, economic, and social union" between the two Germanys is signed.

◄ *At Moscow's 1990 May Day Parade, thousands of demonstrators denounced the Communist government.*

June 1990

On June 12, **Russia** is declared a sovereign state.

On June 20, the Supreme Soviet of **Uzbekistan** declares the republic sovereign.

On June 23, the Supreme Soviet of **Moldavia** adopts a declaration of sovereignty.

On June 29, **Lithuania** suspends its declaration of independence, and Moscow lifts its economic blockade.

On June 10 and 17, free elections are held. The Communist Party, renamed Socialist, receives 47% of the vote.

On June 8-9, the first free elections since 1946 are held. The victors are the Civic Forum in the Czech lands, and its counterpart in **Slovakia**, Public Against Violence, with 47% of the vote. Communists receive almost 14% of the vote.

April 1990

On Apr. 8, the second round of general elections takes place, and the center-right Hungarian Democratic Forum wins 41.6% of the votes.

On Apr. 13, the Soviet authorities admit Soviet responsibility for the Katyn Forest massacre.

On Apr. 19-20, **Solidarity** holds its first major national conference since 1981.

On Apr. 7-8, the NSF meets in its first national conference and calls for a democratic multiparty system.

On Apr. 11, the National Salvation Front bars former King Michael of Romania from entering the country.

On Apr. 8, a center-right coalition called DEMOS wins in the first free elections in **Slovenia**.

On Apr. 22, the first round of elections in **Croatia** takes place.

May 1990

On May 16, Prime Minister Jozsef Antall forms a coalition government.

On May 27, the first fully free elections take place, for local councils. **Solidarity**-backed candidates win 41% of the seats, but only 42% of voters participate in the elections.

On May 20, in the first free elections in Romania since 1937, the National Salvation Front wins 66.3% of the votes, and **Ion Iliescu** wins the presidency with 86% of the votes.

On May 6-7, the second round of general elections takes place in **Croatia**, and the winning party is the right-wing nationalist Croatian Democratic Union.

On May 5, the first round of "two-plus-four" talks on the reunification of **Germany** takes place in Bonn.

On May 29, representatives of 40 countries sign the founding charter of the European Bank for Reconstruction and Development, which is intended to finance the economic rehabilitation of **Eastern Europe**.

June 1990

During June 13-15, violent confrontation takes place in Bucharest between anti-Communist demonstrators and pro-government miners brought into the city. The toll is six people dead and about 500 injured.

Between May 31 and June 3, Presidents **Bush** and **Gorbachev** hold their second summit in Washington.

◄ *In December 1989, dissident playwright Václav Havel was elected president of Czechoslovakia. He received a visit from Pope John Paul II in April 1990.*

	THE SOVIET UNION	ALBANIA	BULGARIA	CZECHOSLOVAKIA	EAST GERMANY
July 1990	On July 10, at the 28th party congress, **Gorbachev** is reelected general secretary. On July 11, **Yeltsin** quits the Communist Party.	In early July, about 5,000 Albanians seek refuge in foreign embassies and are eventually allowed to leave the country. On July 31, Albania and the **U.S.S.R.** restore diplomatic relations.	On July 6, Mladenov is forced to quit because of charges that he wanted to use tanks against demonstrations in December 1989.	On July 6, **Václav Havel** is reelected president for a two-year term.	On July 1, East and West Germany become united economically with one currency. On July 16, seven nations (England, France, the **U.S.**, the U.S.S.R., East Germany, West Germany, and **Poland**) agree on unification of the two Germanys.
Aug. 1990			On Aug. 1, Zhelyu Zhelev, leader of the Union of the Democratic Forces, is elected president.		
Sept. 1990	On Sept. 13, a new German-Soviet friendship pact is signed, allowing the united **Germany** to play a major role in the changing Soviet economy.				
Oct. 1990	On Oct. 1, the U.S.S.R. Supreme Soviet passes a law guaranteeing full religious freedoms. On Oct. 2, **Lithuania** and the U.S.S.R. agree to conduct their economic relations as equal partners. On Oct. 17, the Ukrainian parliament bows to student demands and agrees to support the Ukrainian independence.			On Oct. 11, thousands rally in Prague in an anti-Communist demonstration. On Oct. 17, Finance Minister Václav Klaus is elected chairman of the Civic Forum. He is the most outspoken advocate of free-market economy.	At the stroke of midnight on Oct. 2, East Germany ceases to exist as it voluntarily merges with West Germany. About 1 million people celebrate at the Brandenburg Gate in Berlin.

◄ *In July 1990, thousands of Albanians who had sought refuge in foreign embassies were allowed to leave the country aboard ships sailing under the United Nations flag.*

	THE SOVIET UNION	ALBANIA	BULGARIA	CZECHOSLOVAKIA	EAST GERMANY
Nov. 1990	On Nov. 17, **Gorbachev** presents a new emergency power structure, in which he would rule together with the Federation Council representing the 15 republics. After several days, the plan is rejected by **Yeltsin** as insufficient.		Throughout the month, antigovernment rallies take place in Sofia. The government is forced to resign on Nov. 29.	On Nov. 24, local elections take place; Communists win 17% of the vote.	
Dec. 1990	**Germany** begins airlifting emergency food supplies to the U.S.S.R. On Dec. 20, **Eduard Shevardnadze** resigns, warning of an "onset of dictatorship."	On Dec. 9, a large student demonstration takes place in Tirana.		On Dec. 12, the Federal Assembly approves a new division of power between the Czech lands and **Slovakia**.	

On July 5, **Serbia** suspends the parliament of **Kosovo**.

◄ *On October 2, 1990, amid much celebration, Germany became a united country for the first time since the end of World War II.*

On Aug. 3, the writer Arpád Göncz, member of the Alliance of Free Democrats, is elected Hungarian president.

During Aug. 21-27, antigovernment demonstrations take place in Bucharest.

On Aug. 2, Iraq invades Kuwait.

On Sept. 17, **Wałęsa** declares his presidential cadidacy against **Mazowiecki**.

On Sept. 12, a treaty between WWII Allies and the two Germanys ends the Allied powers' responsibility over **Germany**.

On Oct. 15, the ruling party, Hungarian Democratic Forum, is beaten in local elections. Less than 30% of eligible voters participate.

On Oct. 26, taxi and truck drivers block traffic throughout the country, protesting gas price hikes.

On Oct. 18, the government presents a radical plan for a transition to a market economy.

On December 9, 1990, Lech Wałęsa won the presidency of Poland in a landslide election.
▼

On Nov. 25, **Mazowiecki** resigns after losing the first round of presidential elections.

On Nov. 19, 35 nations, members of the **Conference on Security and Cooperation in Europe** sign a treaty limiting conventional weapons systems in Europe.

On Dec. 9, **Wałęsa** is elected president of Poland in a landslide victory.

On Dec. 2, **Kohl** is elected chancellor of the united **Germany**.

Jan. 1991

THE SOVIET UNION: On January 7, Soviet military forces begin a crackdown in the **Baltic Republics**; 19 people are killed. On January 20, 100,000 people in Moscow protest the intervention.

ALBANIA: The flow of refugees to Greece intensifies in late December and early January.

On January 18, the first legal religious service since 1967 takes place in a Tirana mosque.

CZECHOSLOVAKIA: On January 1, the first package of economic reforms is introduced, including **price liberalization**, "small" **privatization**, and internal convertibility of the Czechoslovak currency.

Feb. 1991

THE SOVIET UNION: On February 9, 90% of voters in **Lithuania** endorse independence.

On February 22, 400,000 people in Moscow protest against censorship.

ALBANIA: Following student strikes and demonstrations, **Ramiz Alia** declares presidential rule on February 20.

BULGARIA: On February 1, the government introduces the first stage of economic reforms by removing price subsidies.

CZECHOSLOVAKIA: On February 10, **Civic Forum**, the opposition coalition that brought down the Communist regime, splits into the rightist Civic Democratic Party and centrist Civic Movement.

EAST GERMANY: In former **East Germany**, unemployment rises to 9% by the end of February.

March 1991

THE SOVIET UNION: In referendums in **Latvia**, **Estonia**, and **Georgia**, most voters support independence.

On March 17, in an all-Union referendum, over 75% of voters agree with the preservation of the U.S.S.R. as a "renewed federation of equal, sovereign republics." Six republics do not participate in the referendum.

ALBANIA: In the first week of March, about 20,000 shipborne Albanians arrive in southern Italian ports.

CZECHOSLOVAKIA: On March 6, **Vladimír Mečiar** founds the Movement for Democratic Slovakia, which aims at greater autonomy for **Slovakia**.

EAST GERMANY: German cabinet approves the "joint program for eastern regeneration," earmarking millions of dollars for the next two years to former **East Germany**.

April 1991

THE SOVIET UNION: On April 23, **Mikhail Gorbachev** and leaders of nine Soviet republics sign a pact paving the way to a new Union treaty and an economic "anti-crisis program."

ALBANIA: On March 31 and April 7, in the first free multiparty elections ever held in the country, the Communist Albanian Party of Labor wins a two-thirds majority in the parliament.

CZECHOSLOVAKIA: On April 23, **Mečiar** is dismissed by the Slovak National Council as head of the Slovak government.

EAST GERMANY: Economic hardships cause a tide of protests in eastern cities. Chancellor **Helmut Kohl** is jeered by several hundred protesters in Erfurt on April 7.

May 1991

THE SOVIET UNION: In late April and May, conflict between **Armenia** and **Azerbaijan** escalates.

On May 26, **Zviad Gamsakhurdia** is elected president of **Georgia**.

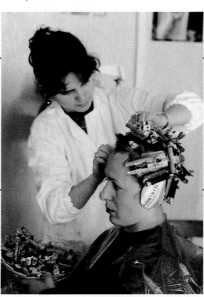

◀ *Private industry has been slow to take hold in formerly hardline Albania. In Tirana, the country's first private hair salon opened in early 1991.*

CZECHOSLOVAKIA: On May 21, the Federal Assembly approves a bill on land **restitution**.

EAST GERMANY: On May 20, four former East German high officials are charged for manslaughter in connection with the Berlin Wall policy of **"shoot-to-kill."**

June 1991

THE SOVIET UNION: On June 12, **Boris Yeltsin** is popularly elected president of **Russia**.

CZECHOSLOVAKIA: By June 30, the last Soviet troops leave Czechoslovakia.

Jan. 1991

Jan Krzysztof Bielecki becomes new premier of Poland.

Anti-government protests that began in mid-December continue throughout January.

On January 14, the constitutional court of Yugoslavia annuls parts of **Slovenia**'s declaration of sovereignty from July 1990.

On January 25, **Macedonia** declares sovereignty.

▲
More than a year after the revolution that led to the execution (above) of Nicolae Ceaușescu, Romania was still beset by much turmoil, and its government remained dominated by former Communists.

Feb. 1991

Railway workers strike throughout February, asking for higher wages.

Energy shortages lead to halting of production in hundreds of enterprises.

On February 20, **Slovenia** initiates "disassociation with Yugoslavia."

March 1991

The Paris Club of 17 creditor countries agrees on March 15 to write off 50% of Poland's debt to foreign governments.

Hundreds of thousands of ▶ mourners turned out to honor the 19 Lithuanians killed when Soviet troops attempted to crack down on the republic's independence movement.

April 1991

Lech Wałęsa travels to Brussels, France, and the United Kingdom to discuss Poland's membership in the European Community.

On April 1, the second stage of the **price liberalization** program starts (the first stage began in November 1990).

President Mitterrand of France travels to Romania, the first Western leader to visit since December 1989.

May 1991

On May 16, the Polish parliament (*Sejm*) rejects an anti-abortion bill. By the end of May, unemployment reaches 7.7%.

On May 10, 12 senior officers of the former *Securitate* Secret Police are sentenced to prison terms between 30 months and five years.

Throughout the month, bloody clashes between Serbs and Croats occur in municipalities in **Croatia** that have a predominantly Serbian population.

June 1991

On June 26, the National Assembly approves a bill that offers partial **compensation** to Hungarians for property nationalized after June 1949.

On June 1, Pope **John Paul II** begins his fourth visit to Poland.

On June 17, Poland and **Germany** sign a friendship treaty.

After **Slovenia** and **Croatia** declare independence on June 25, fighting erupts between the Slovenian Territorial Defence and the Yugoslav National Army.

43

July 1991

On July 1, the **Warsaw Pact** is dissolved in Prague.

On July 12, the Grand National Assembly adopts a new constitution that defines Bulgaria as a "democratic, constitutional, and welfare state."

Aug. 1991

On August 19, Soviet hard-liners depose **Mikhail Gorbachev** and send tanks to major cities to overthrow the democratic forces. **Boris Yeltsin** heads the opposition to the coup. On August 21, **Gorbachev** is reinstated. The Supreme Soviet suspends the Communist Party on August 29. By the end of the month, most Soviet republics declare independence.

On August 7-8, about 10,000 destitute Albanians enter the Italian port of Bari. When Italian authorities try to repatriate the **refugees**, fighting erupts.

◀ *Boris Yeltsin heroically led the opposition to the August 19, 1991, coup by Soviet hard-liners.*

Sept. 1991

State Council of the U.S.S.R. recognizes the independence of **Lithuania**, **Latvia**, and **Estonia**.

Anti-Communist demonstrations continue in Tirana.

In Saxony (former **East Germany**), groups of skinheads and neo-Nazis attack foreigners, mostly from **Romania**, **Yugoslavia**, **Vietnam**, and Africa.

Oct. 1991

On October 13, in the second general elections since the fall of the Communist regime, the opposition Union of Democratic Forces closely defeats the Bulgarian Socialist (formerly Communist) Party.

Nov. 1991

The first completely non-Communist government takes office on November 9.

Dec. 1991

On December 21, the U.S.S.R. is replaced by the **Commonwealth of Independent States (CIS)**, a loose alliance of 11 former Soviet Republics. **Mikhail Gorbachev** resigns on December 25.

▲ *Estonia (above) and its fellow Baltic republics finally gained independence from the Soviet Union in the wake of the botched Moscow coup of August 1991.*

▲ *In the months following German reunification, skinheads and other groups intolerant of foreigners arose in what had been East Germany.*

On December 23, Germany recognizes the independence of **Slovenia** and **Croatia**.

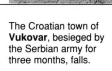

Fighting in **Slovenia** ends on July 3, but violent clashes escalate in eastern **Croatia**.

On July 31, Presidents **George Bush** and **Mikhail Gorbachev** sign the Strategic Arms Reduction Treaty at their third summit meeting in Moscow.

July 1991

Fighting continues in **Croatia**; bombardment of the city of **Vukovar** begins in late August.

Aug. 1991

A brutal civil war began as the various republics that made up Yugoslavia declared their independence. Violent battles took place in many areas of Croatia (above).

On September 26, miners striking against inflation get into a violent conflict with security police in Bucharest; the government subsequently resigns.

Croatia cuts off oil supplies to **Serbia** on September 7. Fighting in **Croatia** continues despite international efforts at mediation.

Sept. 1991

On October 27, free multiparty elections for *Sejm* produce a fragmented legislature; twenty-nine parties are represented, none receiving more than 13% of the vote. Only 43% of eligible voters take part in the elections.

Amid almost constant ▶ bombardment, the people of the Croatian city of Dubrovnik formed long lines to obtain food, water, and other essentials.

Oct. 1991

On November 21, the parliament adopts a new constitution guaranteeing pluralism, human rights, and free markets.

The Croatian town of **Vukovar**, besieged by the Serbian army for three months, falls.

Nov. 1991

On December 7, Hungary becomes the first country to establish full diplomatic relations with **Ukraine**.

On December 5, a new Polish government is formed, headed by Jan Olszewski.

The Maastricht Summit of European Communities, on December 9-10, ends with an agreement on a framework for a European union.

Dec. 1991

45

Jan.-Feb. 1992

Food riots in January and February result in dozens of deaths.

On January 19, **Zhelyu Zhelev** is reelected president for a term of five years.

In early February, the Slovak National Council rejects a draft of the federal constitution.

Tensions with **Czechoslovakia** over the Gabčíkovo hydroelectric dam increase in February.

Wave of strikes protesting price increases sweeps Poland in January.

March-April 1992

On March 22 and 29, the opposition Democratic Party wins in general elections, and, on April 6, **Sali Berisha** becomes Albania's first post-Communist president.

May-June 1992

On May 18, the first round of "large" **privatization** begins.

The June 5-6 general elections result in political polarization between the Czech and Slovak republics.

▲
In March 1992, Roman Petre was confirmed as the president of the National Salvation Front, the party that holds power in Romania. Roman has presided over the country's post-Communist economic reforms.

July-Aug. 1992

▲
In early 1992, Bulgarians reelected Zhelyu Zhelev (above) to the presidency of Bulgaria. The election featured the first large-scale campaigning by candidates in the history of Bulgaria.

On July 17, President **Václav Havel** resigns, after the Slovak National Council adopts a sovereignty declaration.

On July 23, **Václav Klaus** and **Vladimír Mečiar** agree on a plan for peaceful separation of the country.

On August 26, Czech and Slovak leaders agree to divide Czechoslovakia on January 1, 1993.

On July 8, Hanna Suchocka becomes Poland's premier, the first woman premier in the country's history and the fifth premier in the post-Communist period.

Sept.-Oct. 1992

On September 4, ex-leader **Todor Zhivkov** is sentenced to seven years in prison for embezzlement.

The last Russian combat troops leave Poland.

Nov.-Dec. 1992

In June 1992, Alexander ▶ Dubček (left), the chairman of Czechoslovakia's parliament, met with Vladimir Mečiar, the leader of Slovakia's separatist movement.

Economic data show signs of a strong recovery.

46

Jan.-Feb. 1992

The first multiparty local elections take place in February, in three rounds, with the opposition Democratic Convention gaining substantial support.

On January 15, Croatia is recognized by the European Community states. After a cease-fire negotiated in January, U.N. forces are deployed in special areas in February.

Macedonia declares independence in January and is recognized by **Bulgaria**. Slovenia is recognized by the European Community states.

On February 12, **Serbia** and **Montenegro** agree to form a new Yugoslavia.

March-April 1992

On March 29, **Petre Roman** becomes president of the National Salvation Front, which approves his free-market reform program.

On April 25-27, former Romanian king Michael visits the country.

On March 3, Bosnia-Herzegovina's president, **Alija Izetbegović**, proclaims the republic's independence.

By the end of April, more than 400,000 people are left homeless as a result of ethnic violence.

Macedonia and Slovenia establish diplomatic relations on March 17.

Greece refuses to recognize Macedonia because it claims the name "Macedonia" is part of the Greek heritage.

On April 7, **Serbia** and **Montenegro** formally establish a new Yugoslavia.

May-June 1992

On June 1, **privatization** begins in Romania.

During May and June, **Sarajevo** is under intensive attack by the Serbian irregulars, supported by the Yugoslav army. On June 29, U.N. troops take over the **Sarajevo** airport.

◀ *In July 1992, Milan Panić (left), an American citizen, became prime minister of Yugolsavia.*

On May 30, U.N. imposes comprehensive sanctions against Yugoslavia.

On June 28, about 100,000 demonstrators demand the ouster of **Milošević**.

July-Aug. 1992

Fresh military offensives are launched by Serbian forces on July 13.

In August, refugees claim that Serbs have established concentration camps in Serb-held northern Bosnia.

On August 2, **Franjo Tudjman** is reelected to the presidency in direct elections.

Reports of Serbian concentration camps in Bosnia and Herzegovina met with international condemnation. The U.N. also denounced the Serbian policy of "ethnic cleansing."
▼

A Serbian-born U.S. citizen, **Milan Panic**, becomes prime minister of Yugoslavia on July 14.

On August 13, U.N. security resolution condemns the Serbian policy of **"ethnic cleansing."**

Sept.-Oct. 1992

On October 11, **Ion Iliescu** is reelected president.

On September 22, Yugoslavia is expelled from the United Nations.

Nov.-Dec. 1992

Romania replaces **Russia** as the main trading partner of **Moldova**.

On November 20, **NATO** and the Western European Union impose a full naval blockade to enforce a U.N. embargo.

47

	COMMONWEALTH OF INDEPENDENT STATES	RUSSIA	UKRAINE	BELARUS MOLDOVA	ESTONIA LATVIA LITHUANIA
Jan.-Feb. 1992	**Price liberalization** is introduced in most CIS states in early January. Several coordination meetings are held in January and February concerning economic agreements and military affairs.	On January 29, **Boris Yeltsin** issues a decree on accelerating **privatization**. **Yeltsin** visits the **U.S.**, Canada, and France in February.	Ukraine and **Russia** debate the status of **Crimea**.	On January 16, Moldova establishes diplomatic relations with **Hungary**.	On January 25-26, the Interparliamentary Baltic Assembly holds its first meeting.
March-April 1992	On March 13, CIS members agree that an independent agency should administer the former **U.S.S.R.**'s foreign debt.	On March 30, a Federation Treaty is signed by 18 of **Russia**'s 20 autonomous republics. Chechen-Ingushetia and Tatarstan abstain.	On March 1, Ukraine introduces coupons as a new currency.	Fighting in the **Dnestr Republic** leads to the imposition of a state of emergency on March 28.	On March 9, **Latvia** signs an agreement on economic cooperation with **Russia**.
May-June 1992	On May 23, **U.S.** signs a treaty with **Russia**, **Ukraine**, **Belarus**, and **Kazakhstan** on strategic arms reduction.	On June 11, Russia launches the **privatization** of state enterprises.		On May 25, Belarus introduces a new currency called *rubel*. Fighting in **Dnestr Republic** continues in May and June.	
July-Aug. 1992	On August 3, **Boris Yeltsin** of Russia and **Leonid Kravchuk** of **Ukraine** reach an agreement on the Black Sea Fleet.	On July 1, the second stage of the "shock-therapy" economic reform program begins.		On July 7, a cease-fire in the **Dnestr Republic** is negotiated. The Moldovan parliament agrees with the deployment of foreign peace-keeping forces in the region.	Tension grows in the Baltic republics, particularly in **Estonia**, over the continued presence of 130,000 foreign troops. Citizenship laws in **Estonia** and **Latvia** curb the rights of ethnic Russians.
Sept.-Oct. 1992		On September 9, **Boris Yeltsin** postpones a planned trip to Japan, apparently because of domestic pressure from conservatives not to return the Kurile Islands to Japan.	*Since its founding in December 1991, the Commonwealth of Independent States has helped coordinate trade and disarmament policies among the former Soviet republics.* ▼ 		In October, former Communists win Lithuania's first election since independence.
Nov.-Dec. 1992	On November 21, the first group of 100 **U.S.** Peace Corps volunteers arrives in Moscow, part of a wider Peace Corps program to help the former Soviet republics in their transition to democracy.	In early November, **Boris Yeltsin** imposes a state of emergency in north **Ossetia** and Ingushetia in an effort to stop ethnic fighting. At a meeting of the Congress of People's Deputies in early December, **Boris Yeltsin** survives a showdown with hard-liners.			

| AZERBAIJAN ARMENIA | GEORGIA | KAZAKHSTAN KYRGYZSTAN | TAJIKISTAN TURKMENISTAN UZBEKISTAN | OTHER COUNTRIES | |

AZERBAIJAN ARMENIA	GEORGIA	KAZAKHSTAN KYRGYZSTAN	TAJIKISTAN TURKMENISTAN UZBEKISTAN	OTHER COUNTRIES	
During January and February, fighting intensifies in **Nagorny Karabakh**. Armenian attack on the Azerbaijani-inhabited town of Khojali within **Nagorny Karabakh** on February 26-27 leaves hundreds dead.	Armed conflict between supporters and opponents of President **Zviad Gamsakhurdia** leads to the latter's deposition. A military council takes power and, on February 21, restores the constitution from 1921.	On February 24-25, some 17,000 conscripts demonstrate at the Baikonur space center in Kazakhstan in protest against poor living conditions.	On January 16, **price liberalization** leads to riots in Tashkent, Uzbekistan.	Mongolian parliament on January 13 adopts a constitution that renounces socialism and describes **Mongolia** as a republic with parliamentary government. Unemployment in former **East Germany** reaches 17% in January.	Jan.-Feb. 1992
On March 6, Azerbaijan's president Ayaz Mutalibov resigns, accused of failing to defend Azerbaijani lives in **Nagorny Karabakh**.	On March 10, **Eduard Shevardnadze** becomes head of the new State Council. Fighting continues in **Abkhazia** and South **Ossetia**.			◄ *In May 1992, Nursultan Nazarbayev, Kazakhstan's president, met with U.S. President George Bush.*	March-April 1992
On June 7, a staunch nationalist, Abulfaz Elchibey, is elected president of Azerbaijan. He vows never to give up **Nagorny Karabakh**.	On June 24, an agreement between Georgia and **Russia** leads to the stationing of a peace-keeping force in **Ossetia**.	In early May, Kazakhstan concludes a $10 billion deal with Chevron to develop the Tenghiz oil fields.	Anti-Communist demonstrations in Tajikistan lead to the creation of a coalition government on May 12.	On June 28, ex-Communists win in elections in **Mongolia**.	May-June 1992
	Fighting in **Abkhazia** on August 25-26 results in dozens of deaths.			On July 29, **Erich Honecker** is flown to Berlin to face a trial for manslaughter, in connection with the **"shoot-to-kill"** policy of East German regime.	July-Aug. 1992
	◄ *In October 1992, Eduard Shevardnadze, formerly the foreign minister of the Soviet Union, became the Speaker of the Parliament for the republic of Georgia.*		On September 7, Tajikistan's president **Rakhman Nabiyev** is seized by opposition militiamen and forced to resign.	At its 14th congress, the Chinese Communist Party reasserts strict party control in politics, but confirms its support for a free-market economy.	Sept.-Oct. 1992
On November 9, the Azerbaijani air force attacks Stepanakert, the capital of **Nagorny Karabakh**.	On November 11, **Eduard Shevardnadze** inspects **Abkazia**, a region of Georgia troubled by ethnic strife.		On November 16, the Tajik parliament meets to find a solution to the ongoing conflict between pro-government forces and their hard-line Communist opponents.	On November 3, Bill Clinton wins the presidental election in the **United States**.	Nov.-Dec. 1992

49

Even after the fall of Communism, many of the former Eastern Bloc countries remain bleak places to live. Albania (above) remains the poorest country in Europe.

LIFE AFTER COMMUNISM:
An Alphabetical Overview

ABKHAZIA, a small region in northwest **Georgia** on the Black Sea, is one of the hot spots of post-Communist ethnic conflicts. The separatist Turkic-speaking Muslim Abkhaz minority is less than 100,000 strong, but it belongs to a loose alliance of Muslim peoples in the Caucasus who want to throw off the Georgian and Russian rule. Dozens of people were killed in August 1992 during a battle for the Abkhaz capital, Sukhumi.

AFGHANISTAN is a rugged mountainous country located between Pakistan, Central Asia, and Iran. Its 15 million inhabitants form a mosaic of tribal and village units, characterized by strong loyalties and even stronger rivalries. The Soviet invasion of Afghanistan in December 1979 contributed to the collapse of the Communist superpower: it was the first time that Soviet military might did not prevail.

One of the first goals of **Mikhail Gorbachev** was to end the unpopular war. Soviet troops began withdrawing from Afghanistan in 1988 and the last soldiers left by February 15, 1989. A Communist regime survived for three more years, however, and it was only in April 1992 that the *mujaheddin* (Islamic fighters) succeeded in deposing President Najibullah and creating an Islamic state.

ALBANIA, an Alabama-sized country with a population of just over 3 million, is the poorest nation in Europe. Albania borders on **Yugoslavia, Macedonia,** Greece, and the Adriatic Sea.

Despite centuries of foreign rule, Albanians have preserved a separate identity. They gained their independence in 1920, but during World War II were annexed by Italy. Communist guerrillas fought the Italian and German forces and, in 1944, a Communist government led by Enver Hoxha was established.

Between 1946 and 1990, Albania was a harshly ruled Stalinist country. A pervasive **personality cult** surrounded party chief Hoxha until his death in 1985. Professing a fierce self-reliance, Albania early on broke with the **U.S.S.R.** and, later, with **China,** prohibited any borrowing from the West, and, by the end of the 1970s, stood virtually alone in the world. Albanian Communist rulers claimed that their country was the only state truly following the precepts of **Marxism-Leninism.**

The tremors affecting the rest of the Communist world began to shake Albania in early 1990. Demonstrations—something unheard of for the previous 46 years—occurred in Tirana and other Albanian cities that January, spurred on by the events elsewhere in **Eastern Europe,** by economic grievances, and by the weakening grip of the security forces, known as *Sigurimi*. In the spring of 1990, President **Ramiz Alia** announced a program of "democratization," allowing farmers to cultivate private plots, making foreign travel more accessible, and permitting Albanians to practice religious rites in the privacy of their homes.

However welcome this move was, it did not calm the restive population. In July 1990, about 5,000 Albanians stormed foreign embassies and were then allowed to leave the country; many others risked their lives by crossing the borders into **Yugoslavia** and Greece without papers. Unrest continued until, at the end of 1990, the ruling Communist party agreed to multiparty elections, which took place in the spring of 1991. Although the Communists won, mostly because opposition forces were unable to organize properly, anti-Communist rioting led to the formation of a new government in June 1991, which included nine independent members. The next national elections took place in March 1992; this time the opposition Albanian Democratic Party won a landslide victory. Sali Berisha, a 47-year-old heart surgeon, became Albania's first non-Communist president in April 1992.

Meanwhile, the country has been wracked by strikes, riots, and looting. Old vendettas have reemerged, and economic and social chaos has often been almost uncontrollable. After becoming president, Berisha took several trips abroad to ask for foreign aid in order to stabilize the situation.

ALIA, RAMIZ (1925–   ), was the second and final leader of the Albanian Communist Party and president of **Albania** from April 1991 to April 1992. A longtime disciple and follower of his predecessor, **Albania**'s supreme Communist leader Enver Hoxha, Alia tried to remain in power as a reformist, but the historical process swept him away. When the Albanian Democratic Party won in the March 1992 elections, Alia stepped down from the presidency.

ANTISOCIALIST. This term, used from the times of **Stalin,** became especially popular in the 1970s and 1980s, when it was hurled with great gusto at all actual and potential **dissidents,** and at anyone who might even think of disagreeing with the party line.

ARMENIA, a former Soviet republic in the Caucasus, is now an independent country. Landlocked and mountainous, it is slightly larger than Maryland and has about 3.4 million people.

One of the earliest centers of civilization, Armenia became, in the 4th century, the first country to adopt Christianity. After alternating periods of independence and foreign rule (by Turkey and Persia), Armenia became part of the Russian Empire in the early 19th century.

Until **Mikhail Gorbachev** came to power, Armenia was slumbering in the gray uniformity of Soviet life. Since the late 1980s, however, it has become embroiled in a violent ethnic conflict over a region called **Nagorny Karabakh,** which lies within **Azerbaijan** but is inhabited mostly by Armenians. The hostility toward the Azerbaijani has deep historical roots and involves economic, religious, and ethnic differences.

Armenia became independent in late 1991, and it immediately joined the **Commonwealth of Independent States.** Instead of devoting its energies to the building of the new statehood, however, the country has been mired in the escalating conflict with **Azerbaijan.**

AZERBAIJAN, until 1991 a Soviet republic in the Caucasus, is inhabited by a predominantly Muslim population of 6.7 million. The region was ruled by Islamic dynasties from the 7th century onward until the early 19th century, when it became part of the Russian Empire.

Since 1988, Azerbaijan has been involved in a bitter conflict with **Armenia** over a small region within its territory called **Nagorny Karabakh,** which has historical significance for both Armenians and Azerbaijani. The conflict feeds on religious, ethnic, and economic differences between the Christian, Indo-European, and generally more-affluent Armenians, and the Muslim, Turkic, and poorer Azerbaijani.

In January 1990, at least 60 people were killed in an anti-Armenian pogrom in Baku, the Azerbaijan capital. Fighting erupted in several other places, and, on January 19, Soviet troops mounted an assault on Baku. The official death toll was 83, but unofficial sources put the number of people killed as high as 600. At the funeral of the victims of the assault, 750,000 people filled the streets of Baku, and thousands of Azerbaijani party members burned their party membership cards.

Azerbaijan became an independent country in late December 1991, and immediately joined the **Commonwealth of Independent States.** The conflict over **Nagorny Karabakh** escalated in early 1992 and, on March 6 of that year, Azerbaijan's president, Ayaz N. Mutalibov, was forced to resign, accused of taking too soft a stance toward **Armenia.** A small region sandwiched between **Armenia** and Iran, called Nakhichevan, which is a part of Azerbaijan, became involved in the ethnic conflict in May 1992 when **Armenia** launched a full-scale attack on its northern section.

A staunch nationalist and a former opponent of Communism, Abulfaz Elchibey was elected president of Azerbaijan in June 1992.

BALTIC REPUBLICS are three former Soviet republics—**Lithuania, Latvia, and Estonia**—that were forcibly integrated into the **U.S.S.R.** in 1940–41, on the basis of secret protocols appended to the Soviet-Nazi pact of 1939. Following the unsuccessful coup by Soviet hard-liners in August 1991, all three Baltic republics seceded from the **U.S.S.R.** Their independence was recognized by the Kremlin in September.

Ethnic conflicts have erupted in many of the republics that formerly made up the Soviet Union. The strife between Armenia and Azerbaijan has been particularly bitter.

These three republics have been locked in a dispute with **Russia** about the ex-Soviet troops stationed in the area. The withdrawal of the 130,000 military personnel began in February 1992, but then was suspended in October by **Boris Yeltsin,** allegedly because of difficulties in resettling the troops. But the suspension was more likely caused by the tough citizenship laws introduced in **Latvia** and **Estonia,** which reduced the large Russian minorities in these two republics to second-class status.

BELARUS was the third largest republic of the **U.S.S.R.;** until it gained independence in late 1991, it was referred to in Western sources as Belorussia or Byelorussia. The country, a little smaller than Kansas with a population of 10 million, borders **Poland** in the west, **Lithuania** and **Latvia** in the north, **Russia** in the east, and **Ukraine** in the south. The language, Belorussian, is very similar to Russian and Ukrainian; most people use Russian in everyday transactions.

For 28 years, the Berlin Wall divided Communist East Berlin from capitalist West Berlin. West Berliners sometimes gathered at the wall to taunt the East German soldiers.

Belarus is a member of the **Commonwealth of Independent States** and, although independent, it hasn't yet begun to carve a distinct identity of its own.

BERLIN WALL. At the end of World War II, Berlin was partitioned into four sectors, three under the Western Allies and one under the **U.S.S.R.** After the creation of the Federal Republic of Germany and the German Democratic Republic in 1949, Berlin remained divided, but represented a major crack in the **Iron Curtain.** In August 1961, to stop East Germans from fleeing to West Germany, the borders between East and West Berlin were closed and an imposing 5-foot tall concrete wall was erected, topped with broken glass and barbed wire.

On November 9, 1989, with thousands of East Germans beginning to flood the West German embassies in Prague and in Warsaw, the beleaguered East German leadership decided to open the borders. Within a few days, millions of East Germans crossed into West Berlin. A joke at that time told of East German leader **Erich Honecker** waking up at night and finding all East Berlin brightly illuminated but empty; whereupon he went to the Wall and found a note stuck in a crack, with a message, "The last one to leave please put out the lights."

BOSNIA AND HERZEGOVINA became a tragic battlefield in 1992. A former republic of **Yugoslavia,** Bosnia and Herzegovina is a landlocked Balkan country, about the size of New Hampshire and Vermont combined; its 1991 population was 4.5 million. If **Yugoslavia** was a complex mosaic of nationalities and religions, then Bosnia and Herzegovina was a **Yugoslavia** in miniature: about 44 percent of its inhabitants were Muslims— ethnic Slavs who had accepted Islam centuries ago; the second-largest group, about 31 percent, were Eastern Orthodox Serbs; the third group were the Roman Catholic Croats. For decades, these peoples lived in peace, side by side, in hundreds of mixed neighborhoods, villages, and towns. Then, in early 1992, this tranquility suddenly exploded in a fury of violence.

Bosnia and Herzegovina declared independence in March 1992, and almost immediately became embroiled in a brutal conflict between Serbs and Muslims. The Croats originally sided with the latter, but then began to pursue their own goals at the expense of Muslims. In November 1992, the Bosnian government claimed that over 100,000 Bosnian Muslims had been killed since the declaration of independence through the Serbian policy of **"ethnic cleansing."** Thousands of Muslims not killed were driven from their homes by Serbs. The republic's capital, **Sarajevo,** shelled by Serbian guerrillas from the surrounding mountains, came to represent the country's suffering.

Bosnian Serbs set up a "Serbian Republic of Bosnia and Herzegovina" in the northern part of the country and, by late in the summer of 1992, they controlled about two-thirds of the republic's territory. About that time, reports began appearing in the West about Serb-run death camps in the occupied territories. In these camps, hundreds of non-Serbs were being beaten, tortured, and executed.

BRANDT, WILLY (1913–92), was the chancellor of the Federal Republic of Germany (West Germany) from 1969 to 1974. In 1971, he received the Nobel Peace Prize for his policy of opening to the East (the so-called *Ostpolitik*). Brandt was the chief architect of the so-called Basic Treaties that the two Germanies signed in 1972.

BREZHNEV, LEONID (1906–85), was first secretary of the Communist Party of the **U.S.S.R.** from 1964 until his death in 1985. Growing up under **Stalin,**

Brezhnev (left, with West German leader Helmut Schmidt) ruled the Soviet Union for 21 years. The years of his rule are generally considered a period of stagnation.

In August 1990, the Bulgarian parliament chose Zhelyu Zhelev, one of the country's few dissidents during the Communist period, to become president. Zhelev was reelected to a second term in 1992.

he ascended to power after the ouster of **Nikita Khrushchev** in 1964. A conservative hard-liner, he wanted to maintain the status quo at all costs; later, the years of his rule were labeled the "period of stagnation."

During the early 1970s, which saw the beginnings of **détente,** Brezhnev visited the **United States** several times and met with Presidents Nixon and Ford; he also signed the SALT I accord in 1972, limiting antimissile systems and certain offensive weapons. In his final years, he was a pitiful sight: he could barely walk and speak, yet he clung to power until his last breath.

BREZHNEV DOCTRINE was an unofficial policy formulated in the fall of 1968, after the invasion of **Czechoslovakia** by **Warsaw Pact** troops. The doctrine implied that the **U.S.S.R.** could use its armed forces in order to "defend **socialism**" in an allied Communist country.

BULGARIA is a hilly Balkan country that borders the Black Sea in the east, **Romania** in the north, **Yugoslavia** and **Macedonia** in the west, and Greece and Turkey in the south; it is the size of Tennessee, and has a population of about 9 million. The capital, Sofia, was founded by the Romans in the 2nd century. Although the Bulgarians speak a Slavic language, they are the descendants of a mixture of Slavic tribes and central Asian Turkic tribes of Bulgars, who invaded the Balkan Peninsula in the 7th century. The early Bulgarian state adopted Christianity in the 9th century, then came under foreign rule, rose again in the 12th and 13th centuries, but soon after that was conquered by Ottoman Turks. In 1878, Bulgaria became independent thanks to Russian pressure on the Ottomans. The Bulgarians have had a friendly attitude toward **Russia** ever since.

Bulgaria became Communist in 1944, and its party leadership remained unquestionably loyal to Moscow until 1989. Opposition to Communist rule was almost nonexistent.

In his one term, U.S. President George Bush (right) presided over the disintegration of the Soviet Union and met with Russia's first freely elected president, Boris Yeltsin.

In October 1989, a few **dissident** groups held their first rallies while an international conference on the environment took place in Sofia. The presence of foreign delegations compelled the government to show a certain tolerance. On November 3, about 4,000 people demonstrated in front of the National Assembly; it was the largest unofficial demonstration since 1947. On November 10, 1989, the second-longest ruling Eastern European leader, **Todor Zhivkov,** was forced to resign his office.

In January 1990, the government initiated talks with opposition groups, but the opposition was still too immature to present any real challenge to the entrenched establishment. The Communists renamed themselves Socialists and, in free elections in June, won 48 percent of the vote.

Shortly after the elections, hundreds of anti-Communist students built up tents in a "Communist free zone" in Sofia. In August, the Bulgarian parliament chose **Zhelyu Zhelev,** leader of the Union of Democratic Forces and one of a handful of Bulgarian **dissidents,** to become president. In the following months, shortages of virtually everything drove people into the streets in huge demonstrations that forced the government to resign in late November 1990.

Throughout 1991, the strength of the former Communist Party gradually dissipated. In the national elections in October, the opposition Union of Democratic Forces emerged victorious. The first fully democratic government since 1947 was installed.

BUSH, GEORGE (1924–), the forty-first president of the **United States,** presided over the end of the **Cold War.** In the first year and a half of his presidency, he treated the changes in the **U.S.S.R.** and in **Eastern Europe** with extreme caution. Then, in November 1990, at the meeting of the **Conference on Security and Cooperation in Europe,** he declared that the **Cold War** was over.

CEAUŞESCU, NICOLAE (1918–89), was the general secretary of the Romanian Communist Party from 1965 until his death. Ceauşescu began as a Romanian nationalist who won admiration for his defiance of the **U.S.S.R.** in matters of foreign policy. He condemned the invasion of **Czechoslovakia** in 1968 and, in the early 1970s, became a frequent visitor to Western capitals.

Ceauşescu then concentrated on creating a family dynasty. His wife, Elena, despite less than a high-school education, became the head of the National Council for Science and Technology, and was increasingly praised as one of the world's leading scientists; his brothers and children were also placed in high positions.

In 1982, Ceauşescu's decision to pay off all foreign debt plunged **Romania** into both virtual and metaphorical darkness (only very low-watt bulbs were permitted). At the same time, he began to build in downtown Bucharest a mammoth marble-covered palace, with thousands of rooms and such extravaganzas as a 980-bulb chandelier. While the Romanian people had barely enough to eat and shivered in their unheated apartments, Ceauşescu devoted time every Saturday to pester architects at the building site of the grandiose structure. In the last years of his rule, his megalomania and obsession with absolute power apparently made him lose touch with reality.

The dramatic demise of Ceauşescu was seen by millions of television viewers around the world: his utter disbelief when he was heckled during an official rally on December 20, 1989; his defiance at the hastily arranged trial several days later; and finally his crumpled body minutes after the execution on December 25.

CHINA is the most populous country on Earth: every fifth inhabitant of this planet is Chinese. China became a Communist power in 1947, under Chairman Mao Tse-Tung. Since that time, the country has gone through several major upheavals. During the *Great Leap Forward,* Chinese farm-

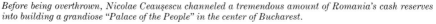
Before being overthrown, Nicolae Ceauşescu channeled a tremendous amount of Romania's cash reserves into building a grandiose "Palace of the People" in the center of Bucharest.

China's aging leadership remains fully committed to the hard-line Communist line. Nonetheless, the government is allowing some experimentation with free enterprise.

ers were exhorted to build backyard furnaces to increase steel production and so catch up with Great Britain. The hectic industrialization drive backfired and Mao had to recapture his stature by launching the *Cultural Revolution* of the late 1960s, during which millions of frenzied young students marched through Chinese cities and hunted down **counterrevolutionaries.**

After Mao's death in 1976, the new Chinese leadership under the pragmatic Teng Hsiao-P'ing began to modernize the country and permit quite a few "capitalist" practices, including the **privatization** of agriculture. In contrast to the developments in the **U.S.S.R.,** however, political power has remained with the Communist Party. When students challenged the Communist iron grip on power through pro-democracy demonstrations in Beijing's Tiananmen Square, the aging leadership suppressed the demonstrators with great brutality. Many secret trials of **dissidents** took place in the following years.

CHARTER 77 was the name of a manifesto issued by a group of 242 Czech and Slovak **dissidents** in early January 1977: among its first signatories was the future president of **Czechoslovakia, Václav Havel.** The manifesto listed some basic human rights demands. Although it was worded in cautious language, Charter 77 provoked a furious backlash from the authorities. Signatories were arrested, forced into exile, or otherwise harassed; nonetheless, the core group formed at that time remained the nucleus of the Czechoslovakian **dissident** movement for the next 12 years. In November 1992, Charter 77 was disbanded because its founders decided that it had "fulfilled its function."

COLD WAR. During World War II, the **U.S.S.R.** was one of the four major Allies who fought against **Germany.** Signs of tensions between the **U.S.S.R.** and the West appeared as early as late 1945 and soon developed into a full-blown break. During the following four decades, the Cold War

In a sure sign that Cold War tensions had eased, the Soviet Union gradually withdrew its troops from Eastern Europe after its former satellite countries rejected Communism.

was most clearly manifested in regional conflicts—whenever something happened in the world, the **United States** and the Soviet Union were always on opposite sides. The Cold War was at its most intense in the early 1950s; later, antagonism alternated with periods of more-friendly relations, particularly the **détente** during the 1970s. After the **U.S.S.R.** invaded **Afghanistan** in December 1979, the relations between the superpowers turned hostile again.

By the end of 1990, the Cold War had been officially proclaimed dead. The first test of the new world order has been the crisis in the Middle East, after Iraq invaded Kuwait in August 1990: it was the first time since World War II that the **U.S.S.R.** and the **U.S.** stood on the same side during a regional conflict.

COMECON, or CMEA (Council for Mutual Economic Assistance), was an economic grouping of Communist countries founded in 1949. By the 1980s, its members included **Bulgaria, Czechoslovakia, East Germany, Hungary, Poland, Romania,** and the **U.S.S.R.** (**Albania** was a member from 1949 to 1968). Non-European members were **Cuba, Mongolia,** and **Vietnam.** COMECON was intended to promote the "socialist economic organization," but its only achievement was to ensure a sufficient flow of cheap oil and raw materials from the **U.S.S.R.** to **Eastern Europe.** COMECON disbanded in June 1991.

COMMONWEALTH OF INDEPENDENT STATES was first established by the leaders of **Russia, Ukraine,** and **Belarus** on December 8, 1991, in Minsk, the capital of **Belarus.** These leaders announced that they considered the **U.S.S.R.** defunct and that they therefore created a new body which was open to all former Soviet republics. On December 21, 1991, the three original founders of CIS were joined at Alma Ata (the capital of **Kazakhstan**) by the leaders of **Kazakhstan, Kyrgyzstan, Tajikistan, Turkmenistan, Uzbekistan, Moldova, Armenia,** and **Azerbaijan.** The **Baltic Republics** did not join CIS, and neither did **Georgia,** which at the time was convulsed by the struggle between supporters and opponents of President **Zviad Gamsakhurdia.** The CIS pledged to continue the Soviet Union's policy of disarmament. The first and last Soviet president, **Mikhail Gorbachev,** resigned on December 25, 1991, and handed over the nuclear codes to the president of Russia, **Boris Yeltsin.**

A number of summit meetings of CIS member states took place throughout 1992, and many agreements on economic and political cooperation and coordination were signed. In October 1992, **Azerbaijan** left the Commonwealth.

COMMUNISM is a word dating from the mid-19th century. The vision of Communism as a classless, economically just society was first formulated by Karl Marx in his *Communist Manifesto* of 1848. The first sentence of the booklet read, "The specter of Communism is stalking Europe," and it proved to be correct, albeit in a different way than Marx had in mind. The manifesto concluded with a ringing appeal, "Workers of the world, unite!," a phrase that later became one of the magic formulas of the Communist world. In a bitter joke, one banner at the unofficial rally during Moscow's 72nd anniversary celebration of the **October Revolution** in 1989 carried a paraphrase, "Workers of the world, forgive us."

CONFERENCE ON SECURITY AND COOPERATION IN EUROPE grew out of the **Helsinki Accords,** signed by 35 countries in 1975. The crowning achievement of the conference is the treaty limiting conventional weapons systems in Europe, concluded in Paris on November 19, 1990.

In July 1992, a two-day summit in Helsinki, the largest gathering of government leaders ever held in Europe, dealt with the Balkan crisis. Despite urgent calls from Bosnian President **Alija Izetbegović** for military intervention in **Bosnia and Herzegovina,** the participants only agreed to blame the "authorities in Belgrade" for the violence, but did not agree to take any concrete steps.

COUNTERREVOLUTIONARY was a very strong and inflammatory term—stronger than **antisocialist,** to label the opponents and critics of the Communist regimes.

CRIMEA, a peninsula jutting into the Black Sea, became part of **Russia** in the late 18th century. In 1954, **Nikita Khrushchev** "gave" Crimea to **Ukraine,** as an expression of the friendship between the peoples of these two Soviet republics. At that time, it was an empty gesture, because everything was decided in Moscow anyway. But in 1991, when the **U.S.S.R.** disintegrated and **Russia** and **Ukraine** became independent nations, the status of Crimea began to cause problems. Not only are most inhabitants ethnic Russians, but the Crimean port of Sevastopol is home to the Black Sea Fleet, consisting of about 350 ships and 70,000 sailors. In August 1992, **Boris Yeltsin** of **Russia** and **Leonid Kravchuk** of **Ukraine** agreed that the fleet would remain for three years under joint control and then would be divided between **Russia** and **Ukraine.**

CROATIA, one of the six former constituent republics of **Yugoslavia,** is twice as large as Maryland and has about 4.6 million people, 11 percent

Fidel Castro has ruled Cuba since the Communist takeover in 1959. With the collapse of the Soviet Union and the fall of Eastern European Communism, Castro has lost his main sources of support.

of whom are ethnic Serbs. Croats are Roman Catholics, use the Latin script, and have for centuries considered themselves part of Western Christendom.

In the spring of 1990, Croatia's first free elections were won by a nationalist right-of-center party, the Croatian Democratic Union. The next year, in June 1991, Croatia declared independence, which immediately provoked violent conflict in areas inhabited mostly by Serbs. By the end of the year, about one-third of Croatian territory had been overrun and lost to Serbs, and some 50,000 Croats fled to **Hungary.** After dozens of cease-fires negotiated by the United Nations and the European Community had been broken, the fighting finally subsided and U.N. peace-keeping forces were deployed in the contested areas of Croatia in early 1992. About 12,000 U.N. Protection Forces were stationed in Croatia in September 1992.

CUBA, an island country less than 100 miles off the coast of Florida, has been under the rule of Fidel Castro since January 1959; it is now one of the last staunchly Communist countries in the world. The loss of economic support from the **U.S.S.R.** and **Eastern Europe** has caused tremendous hardships for Cuba, but Castro is still adamant in his strident hostility to the **United States** and in his relentless opposition to any challenge to one-party rule.

CZECHOSLOVAKIA was for most of the 20th century a country in the center of Europe, but in January 1993 it split into two parts, the **Czech Republic** and **Slovakia.** Rising from the ashes of the Austro-Hungarian Empire at the end of World War I, Czechoslovakia combined the historic lands of Bohemia and Moravia with **Slovakia,** inhabited by Slovaks, close linguistic cousins of Czechs and Moravians. Until 1938, Czechoslovakia was a well-functioning progressive liberal democracy, but it disintegrated under the onslaught of Nazism.

Communist rule was established in February 1948, and Stalinist regimes persisted into the early 1960s. Then, jolted by a sudden economic crisis, the leadership embarked on economic reforms and also began to introduce political liberalization. This gradual reformist process culminated in the **Prague Spring** of 1968, led by the reformist Communists headed by **Alexander Dubček.** This eight-month period was crushed by a **Warsaw Pact** invasion in August 1968.

The new hard-line leadership, under Gustáv Husák, purged the party of everyone even remotely suspected of reformist inclinations and the country plunged into a stuporous period of "normalization," during which most people retreated into a private "exile" of purely personal concerns. Only a handful of brave men and women, loosely grouped around the **Charter 77** movement, opposed the repression.

The country first stirred from its slumber on August 21, 1988, the 20th anniversary of the **Warsaw Pact** invasion of 1968: about 20,000 demonstrators surprised the police and everyone else. It took 15 more months and a number of other demonstrations, petitions, and additional acts of defiance to finally culminate in the "velvet revolution" of November-December 1989. The brutal beating of students on November 17 was the straw that broke the camel's back. Within a few weeks, the top of the Communist pyramid, no longer supported by Soviet tanks, fell off. On December 10, the country had its first predominantly non-Communist government since 1948. Later in the month, the dissident playwright **Václav Havel** was elected president.

In Prague, citizens have eagerly embraced the less-restrictive post-Communist atmosphere.

By the end of 1990, the exhilaration triggered by the newly won freedoms had been replaced by the everyday reality of problems looming ahead: how to eliminate the surviving **nomenclature** in high economic posts; how to dismantle the complex system of command economy; and how to solve the nationalist tensions with **Slovakia.** The latter problem escalated in 1991 and 1992 and finally led to the splitting of Czechoslovakia in January 1993; the process has been peaceful.

CZECH REPUBLIC is a new country created in 1993 from the western part of **Czechoslovakia.** About the size of South Carolina and with a population of 10 million, it consists of two historic regions, Bohemia in the west and Moravia in the east. From the 10th century until 1806, Bohemia and Moravia were autonomous political entities within the Holy Roman Empire; they later became part of the Austro-Hungarian Empire.

DE-STALINIZATION was initiated by **Nikita Khrushchev** shortly after his "secret speech" in February 1956 in which he denounced **Stalin**'s reign of terror. For millions of people both in the **U.S.S.R.** and abroad, **Stalin** had been a supreme hero, and so **Khrushchev**'s revelations came as a tremendous shock. The "secret speech" was not published in the Soviet Union until early 1989.

Khrushchev's de-Stalinization consisted mostly of the following:

● The vast prison system, or gulag—as later described by **Alexander Solzhenitsyn**—was largely dismantled, and thousands of prisoners were released.

● A cultural "thaw" (or liberalization) was introduced, which permitted the publishing of unorthodox authors.

● The **personality cult** was gradually eliminated.

● Dialogue with the West was initiated, and **Khrushchev** became the first Soviet leader to visit the **United States.**

DÉTENTE, which means relaxing of political tensions between countries, started in 1970 when **Willy Brandt** embarked on his policy of conciliation with **East Germany.** Then, in 1972, **U.S.** President Richard Nixon visited **China** and the **U.S.S.R.,** and **Leonid Brezhnev** had several summit meetings with American and West European leaders. The détente culminated in the **Helsinki Accords** of 1975 and ended with the Soviet invasion of **Afghanistan** in December 1979.

DISSIDENT, to designate a dissenting individual or group in Communist countries, is a term that came into general use in the 1970s. Dissidents were harassed, accused of **antisocialist** acts, sometimes put in prison, and later often exiled to the West. The most famous case was the forced exile of **Alexander Solzhenitsyn** in early 1974. All the dissident movements, with the exception of Polish **Solidarity,** were numerically small, but they represented the seeds of the forthcoming revolutionary upheaval. Some former dissidents are now presidents, prime ministers, and high officials in the new Eastern European and Soviet governments.

DNESTR REPUBLIC, or more precisely, Trans-Dniester Republic, is a narrow strip of land along the left bank on the River Dnestr in eastern **Moldova.** In 1992, it became one of the hot-spots of nationalist tensions within the former **U.S.S.R.** The Slavic inhabitants of this area, fearing the domination of ethnically Romanian Moldovans, declared independence in late 1991. Fighting between the Dnestr National Guard and the Moldovan police erupted in March 1992 and continued for several months, claiming many lives. A peacekeeping force of the **Commonwealth of Independent States,** deployed in the region in late summer of 1992, has helped reduce tensions.

DUBČEK, ALEXANDER (1921–92), known in the West as the leader of the **Prague Spring,** was born a few months after his parents had returned from Chicago to their native **Slovakia,** and then spent his youth in the **U.S.S.R.** In early 1968, when he announced his program of "**socialism** with a human face," Dubček turned into a symbol of hope during the euphoric eight-month liberalization period. After August 1968, he was expelled from the party and made a "nonperson."

During the "velvet revolution" in November 1989, he came to Prague, and then became the chairman of the Federal Assembly. He died from injuries incurred in a car accident.

EASTERN EUROPE. This term was used to designate the European Communist countries, but since Europe extends from the Atlantic in the west to the Ural Mountains in the east, "Eastern Europe" is a misnomer: **Poland,** the **Czech Republic, Slovakia, Hungary,** and the former **East Germany** lie in the center of Europe. People in these countries have always felt that they belong to Western European civilization.

The southern four countries belonging to the political group of "Eastern Europe"—**Romania, Bulgaria, Yugoslavia,** and **Albania**—are more properly the Balkan countries, which historically have composed that part of southern Europe influenced by Orthodox Christianity and the Ottoman Empire.

EAST GERMANY was a Communist German state known formally as the German Democratic Republic, which lasted from October 7, 1949, until October 2, 1990–40 years and 360 days. Almost the same size as Tennessee, the country had 16 million people.

In 1945, the defeated Nazi **Germany** was divided into four occupation zones, and as the World War II Allies—the **United States,** Britain, France, and the **U.S.S.R.**—drifted apart in the first years of the **Cold War,** the three western zones were combined into the Federal Republic of Germany in 1949. Shortly after that, the eastern zone, administered by the **U.S.S.R.,** was constituted into the German Democratic Republic.

The first half of East German existence, linked with the tenure of the hard-liner Walter Ulbricht, was characterized by a stringent hostility to-

After the Berlin Wall came down, East Germans making their first excursions into the West were amazed at the variety and abundance of consumer goods available.

ward West Germany, culminating in the erection of the **Berlin Wall** in 1961. The second half, under the leadership of **Erich Honecker,** was ushered in by **Willy Brandt**'s "Ostpolitik," a policy of conciliation between the two German states.

Economically better off than people in other Communist states, East Germans had two major grievances: they were constantly comparing themselves to their wealthier West German kin, and they bitterly resented the impossibility of foreign travel. It was not really surprising that when the **Iron Curtain** along the Austro-Hungarian border cracked in the summer of 1989, East Germans started pouring through. Their dramatic exodus, initially across **Hungary** and later through West German embassies in Prague and Warsaw, was followed by millions of television viewers throughout the world.

During September 1989, growing numbers of demonstrators in East German cities began to chant "We want to stay," and demanded changes. **Erich Honecker** resigned on October 18 and was replaced by Egon Krenz, who had his moment of glory on November 9, when he ordered the **Berlin Wall** opened. After several months of political turmoil, the first free East German elections took place in March 1990. The Christian Democratic Union (a newly formed sister party of the West German Christian Democrats) captured 41 percent of the vote.

Meanwhile, West German Chancellor **Helmut Kohl** was energetically pursuing his plan for reunification. In March, the "two plus four" (two Germanies plus the **U.S.,** Britain, France, and the **U.S.S.R.**) talks on reunification opened in Bonn, and on September 12, 1990, the *Final Settlement with Respect to Germany* was signed by the victorious World War II Allies and by the two Germanies. It was the formal end of World War II.

This treaty opened the way to German reunification, which took effect at midnight on October 2, 1990. East Germany ceased to exist, and was incorporated—as five newly constituted states—into the Federal Republic of **Germany.**

ESTONIA, the northernmost of the three **Baltic Republics,** is about twice the size of Massachusetts. The republic has 1.6 million inhabitants, but only 62 percent of them are ethnic Estonians, who speak an Ugro-Finnic language related to Finnish and Hungarian. The most Western of all former Soviet republics, Estonia has a Scandinavian look and atmosphere.

On its road to independence, Estonia was spared violent confrontation with Soviet troops, in contrast to **Lithuania** and **Latvia.** The country was recognized by Moscow as a sovereign state in September 1991.

A citizenship law adopted in 1992 granted automatic citizenship only to those inhabitants of Estonia, or their descendants, who had lived there before the 1940 annexation by the Soviet Union. This excluded most of the ethnic Russians from citizenship; they can apply for citizenship, but the process takes three years. This issue has contributed to the tensions with **Russia** over the withdrawal of troops from the Baltic region.

ETHNIC CLEANSING is the term used by Serbians for forced evacuations of non-Serb inhabitants from the captured areas in **Bosnia and Herzegovina** and creation of "ethnically pure" regions. The policy was unanimously condemned by a U.N. Security Council resolution in August 1992.

In parts of Bosnia and Herzegovina, the Serbian militia have set up concentration camps (above) and removed non-Serbian residents in a policy called "ethnic cleansing."

GAMSAKHURDIA, ZVIAD K. (1939–   ), president of **Georgia** between May 1991 and January 1992, was the first popularly elected head of a Soviet republic. A former active **dissident,** Gamsakhurdia was accused by his critics of trying to establish a dictatorship. Fighting broke out between his followers and opponents in the summer of 1990, leaving about 100 people dead. Gamsakhurdia was defeated in late 1991 and fled Tbilisi, **Georgia**'s capital, on January 6, 1992. His supporters tried another coup in June 1992 by taking over a broadcasting center in Tbilisi, but were routed by government forces. Gamsakhurdia was later replaced by **Eduard Shevardnadze.**

GEORGIA, formerly a Soviet republic, is located in the Caucasus, a mountainous divide between Europe and Asia. It is somewhat larger than West Virginia and its 5 million inhabitants are proud heirs of a more than 2,000-year-old history. The most famous (or rather infamous) Georgian was Josif Vissarionovich Dzhugashvili, who early in his career adopted the pseudonym **Stalin.**

In April 1989, Soviet troops attacked a nationalist demonstration in the Georgian capital, Tbilisi, and clubbed 20 people to death. The troops also used toxic gas. This event shocked the Georgian people and led to even greater agitation for independence from the Soviet Union. Ethnic conflicts with inhabitants of **Abkhazia,** a region in northwest Georgia, developed in 1989 and have continued ever since; another site of ethnic violence is South **Ossetia.**

The first popularly elected leader of a Soviet republic was the Georgian nationalist **Zviad Gamsakhurdia,** who became the republic's president in May 1991. **Gamsakhurdia** was deposed in January 1992, and after an interim period was replaced by **Eduard Shevardnadze.**

In 1989, East and West Germans gathered triumphantly on the crumbling Berlin Wall. The euphoria was short-lived, however, as the country faced the problems associated with reunification.

GERMANY is the wealthiest and most populous country in Europe, with 77.5 million inhabitants. Germans, like the French, trace the beginnings of their political history to Charlemagne. But in contrast to the French, the Germans were first unified into one state only in 1871. During the Middle Ages and early modern period, the present-day Germany consisted of a multitude of small principalities, which had been part of the Holy Roman Empire (together with most of Italy, Austria, Bohemia, and other regions). "The Iron Chancellor" Otto Bismarck, a Prussian statesman, engineered German unification in the late 19th century. The new state, eager to take its place alongside the major European powers, soon began to pursue an aggressive expansionist policy, which in several decades led to the outbreak of World War I (in 1914). Crushed in a humiliating defeat, Germany tried after the war to rebound, but was hampered by the burden of reparations combined with worldwide economic depression. Dissatisfied, frustrated, and looking for change, many Germans voted for Adolf Hitler in 1933.

After World War II, Germany was divided into Communist **East Germany** and the democratic Federal Republic of Germany (West Germany). The second German unification, made possible by the collapse of

Communist rule in **Eastern Europe,** created a powerful new country in the heart of the continent. By late 1992, many people both inside and outside Germany had begun to doubt the wisdom of the speed with which the two Germanies were made one country again. The costs of unification are proving much higher than originally estimated and tensions between former East Germans and their Western relatives are now a far cry from the euphoric moments after the breaching of the **Berlin Wall.**

In addition, many Europeans worry about the nefarious legacies of the German past. Despite the democratic achievements of postwar West Germany, doubts persist—particularly among the older generations. The increasing right-wing anti-**refugee** violence has contributed to these apprehensions.

GLASNOST, a term introduced by **Mikhail Gorbachev,** became a household word throughout most of the world in the late 1980s. Meaning "openness," it referred mainly to the open public debate about social, political, and economic matters, and about the country's past. In many ways, glasnost was a traumatic experience for Soviet citizens, especially the older ones, because it undermined virtually all certainties and rules.

Conceived as one of the means to achieve **perestroika,** a transformation of the Soviet system, glasnost was ultimately one of the agents leading to the collapse of the **U.S.S.R.**

GORBACHEV, MIKHAIL (1931–   ), the last Soviet leader, was general secretary of the Communist Party of the **U.S.S.R.** from March 1985 to August 1991, president of the **U.S.S.R.** from March 1990 to December 1991, and a Nobel Peace Prize winner in 1990. Well-educated and a forceful personality, Gorbachev differed from all the previous Soviet rulers in several aspects: he did not share their distrust or fear of the West; he was no dogmatist and no dictator; and he was willing to learn from his mistakes. Ultimately, however, he became a victim of his inbred Communist past and ways of thinking—especially after the failed coup of August 1991. He opened the door but then hesitated. It was his rival and opponent, **Boris Yeltsin,** who crossed the threshold into the new era.

Mikhail Gorbachev's policies set in motion the events that led to the fall of Communism.

HAVEL, VÁCLAV (1937–   ), playwright, writer, and the last president of **Czechoslovakia** (from December 1989 to July 1992). Born into a wealthy family, Havel was not admitted to a secondary school because he was branded a "class enemy." One of the founders of the **Charter 77** movement, he spent over four years in prison, the last time in the spring of

Václav Havel, a prominent dissident during Czechoslovakia's Communist period, became president after the country's "velvet revolution." He resigned the post in July 1992.

1989. In November of that year, Havel led the Czechoslovak "velvet rev-olution" as head of the Civic Forum, and, in December, was elected president of the country. Havel was reelected to a two-year term in July 1990, and he vainly tried to maintain **Czechoslovakia** as one state. After the June 1992 elections, the Slovak leader **Vladimír Mečiar** blocked Hav-el's reelection to the presidency. When **Slovakia** declared its sovereignty in July, Havel resigned.

HELSINKI ACCORDS were the first document of the **Conference on Secu-rity and Cooperation in Europe,** signed in 1975 in Helsinki, Finland. The document guaranteed the inviolability of European borders and included pledges to respect human rights. In late 1970, dissident "Helsinki groups" emerged in many Communist countries and demanded from their governments respect for human rights.

HONECKER, ERICH (1912–), was the leader of the East German Com-munist Party from 1971, and head of **East Germany** as chairman of the State Council until he was deposed in October 1989. He presided over a conciliation between the two Germanies and, in 1987, became the first East German head of state to visit West Germany. When **Mikhail Gor-bachev** shook the Communist world with his calls for change, Honecker claimed that **East Germany** did not need any reforms.

In March 1991, after the reunification of **Germany,** Honecker fled to Moscow, finding asylum in the Chilean embassy there. But on July 29, 1992, he was flown to Berlin to face charges of misappropriation of state funds and manslaughter, the latter in connection with the **"shoot-to-kill"** policy of the East German government.

HUNGARY is a flat, landlocked country in the center of Europe, some-what smaller than Indiana. Its 10 million inhabitants are descendants of warrior-nomad Magyar tribes that came to central Europe from Asia in the 9th century. Gradually, they settled down, accepted Christianity, and formed an important medieval kingdom.

In the 19th century, Hungary gained internal autonomy within the Austro-Hungarian Empire. When the empire collapsed at the end of World War I, Hungary lost about two-thirds of its territory to the newly formed **Czechoslovakia,** to **Romania,** and to **Yugoslavia.** Significant Hungarian minorities continue to live in those countries, the largest being in Romanian Transylvania.

In 1941, Hungary joined World War II on the side of **Germany.** After the war, the Hungarian Communists took power with the help of the Soviet occupying forces. An anti-Communist and anti-Soviet resentment persisted, which finally, in 1956, grew into an open revolt. In early November, the uprising was brutally suppressed by Soviet forces: the estimates of people killed range from 6,500 to 32,000. About 250 participants, including the hero of the uprising, Imre Nagy, were later executed.

Then began the era of **János Kádár,** who was installed as premier by the Soviets. Hated at that time, he later began to implement political and economic reforms and gained much respect for his policies. The Hungarian system, branded by **Nikita Khrushchev** as "goulash **Communism,"** gradually evolved into one of the most liberal Communist regimes.

In the late 1980s, the authority of the Hungarian Communist Party began to erode. In June 1989, the party leadership initiated round-table talks with the main opposition groups. Around that time, an official re-evaluation of the 1956 uprising took place, and it was no longer called a **"counterrevolution."** In October, the Hungarian Communist Party was dissolved and reconstituted as the Hungarian Socialist Party. At the same time, opposition forces crystallized into several distinct groupings, the major ones being the Hungarian Democratic Forum (appealing to nationalist Hungarian sentiments) and the Alliance of Free Democrats (representing urban intellectuals and former dissidents).

Meanwhile, Hungary opened its borders with Austria in the summer of 1989, and thousands of East Germans vacationing in the country de-

Perhaps because of its pre-1989 system of "goulash Communism," Hungary never seemed to suffer from the shortages of fresh fruit, vegetables, and other foods that beset its neighbors.

As Polish prime minister, Wojciech Jaruzelski (center, at a wreath-laying ceremony) led the 1981 crackdown on Solidarity, in part to avoid possible Soviet military intervention.

cided to head west. This movement grew like an avalanche and, within a few months, mushroomed into the final fatal crisis of hard-line Eastern European Communist regimes.

Hungarians might have felt a little cheated because their transition to the post-Communist era has been relatively quiet and undramatic. The first free elections since 1946 took place in March and April 1990, and the Hungarian Democratic Forum emerged as winner. The reformed Communists received only 11 percent of the vote. Since 1990, Hungary has steadily pursued its economic transformation, including **privatization** of state enterprises and return of land to private farmers.

ILIESCU, ION (1930–   ), leader of the Romanian National Salvation Front, was elected president of **Romania** in May 1990, with 85 percent of the vote. Iliescu had studied in Moscow, and then held senior posts in regional administration, but in the 1980s was pushed aside by **Nicolae Ceauşescu.** Although the antigovernment opponents have repeatedly charged that Iliescu's commitment to democracy and market economy was not sincere, Iliescu was nonetheless elected by a 60 percent majority to his second presidential term in October 1992.

IRON CURTAIN. In a speech in Missouri on March 15, 1946, Sir Winston Churchill said that "an Iron Curtain has descended over the continent." Thus was coined the term that for decades would describe the heavily fortified and virtually impenetrable border between the West and the Communist countries. The Iron Curtain stretched from the Baltic Sea in the north to Trieste, **Yugoslavia,** in the south. A new part was added in 1961, with the erection of the **Berlin Wall.**

IZETBEGOVIĆ, ALIJA, has been the president of independent **Bosnia and Herzegovina** since March 1992. He has repeatedly called for Western military intervention in his country to stop the onslaught of Bosnian Serbs, but to no avail.

JARUZELSKI, WOJCIECH (1923–   ), general of the Polish army, became prime minister of **Poland** in March 1981, during the heyday of **Solidarity.** Under intense Soviet pressure to do something about the **antisocialist** forces in the country, he declared martial law in December 1981 and had the **Solidarity** leaders and activists arrested, including **Lech Wałęsa.** In July 1989, Jaruzelski was elected president of **Poland,** a position he retained until the presidential elections in November 1990.

JOHN PAUL II (1920–   ). Karol Wojtyła, archbishop of Cracow, was elevated to the papacy in 1978, the first Slavic pope ever to occupy the highest post in the Roman Catholic Church. He greatly contributed to the determination of his Polish compatriots to challenge **Communism.**

In December 1989, John Paul II had a 75-minute private audience with **Mikhail Gorbachev,** the first meeting ever between a pope and a Soviet leader. When **Stalin,** dismissing the church as totally irrelevant, sarcastically asked, "How many divisions does the pope have?," he would have been appalled if he could have envisioned this meeting.

KÁDÁR, JÁNOS (1912–89), was the Hungarian Communist leader between 1956 and 1988. Coming to power during the 1956 uprising, with Soviet backing, Kádár became known as the "butcher of Budapest." In 1961, however, he put forward the slogan, "Whoever is not against us is with us," and thus initiated a period of national conciliation. A sweeping amnesty in 1962 and subsequent economic liberalizations made **Hungary** the most liberal country in **Eastern Europe.**

In the late 1980s, however, Kádár became increasingly resistant to reforms and, in May 1988, was "kicked upstairs" to the largely ceremonial post of party president.

KAZAKHSTAN, a newly independent Central Asian republic, is four times the size of Texas and has a population of 16 million. Part of the **U.S.S.R.**

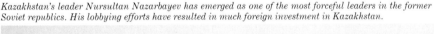

Kazakhstan's leader Nursultan Nazarbayev has emerged as one of the most forceful leaders in the former Soviet republics. His lobbying efforts have resulted in much foreign investment in Kazakhstan.

until 1991, Kazakhstan is one of the four former Soviet republics with nuclear weapons located within its borders. The space center at Baikonur will continue to be used by the **Commonwealth of Independent States.**

Historically a land of nomadic horsemen, Kazakhstan was transformed during the Soviet period into a country with huge cotton plantations and heavily polluted industrial urban centers. The republic's leader, **Nursultan Nazarbayev,** has emerged as one of the more forceful post-Communist rulers. In May 1992, during a visit to the **United States, Nazarbayev** signed a multi-billion dollar investment deal with the **U.S.** oil company Chevron, for the development of the enormous Tenghiz oil fields near the Caspian Sea.

KHRUSHCHEV, NIKITA (1894–71), a Soviet leader who began his political career under **Stalin,** shocked the Soviet Communist Party—and the rest of the world—after the dictator's death with his "Secret Speech" of February 1956. In the speech, Khrushchev denounced **Stalin**'s crimes and initiated the period of **de-Stalinization.** A timid precursor of **Mikhail Gorbachev,** Khrushchev was forced out of office in 1964. In the last years of his life, he secretly dictated his memoirs, which appeared in the West.

KLAUS, VÁCLAV (1941–   ), prime minister of the **Czech Republic** from January 1993, and leader of the center-right Civic Democratic Party. Klaus emerged as a forceful politician in 1990 and became known in the West as the architect of the coupon **privatization** system. He is a very capable economist, but insiders complain about his aggressive personality.

KOHL, HELMUT (1930–   ), West German chancellor and the architect of German reunification. One of Kohl's greatest moments was in July 1990, when he emerged from a meeting with **Mikhail Gorbachev** and announced that the **U.S.S.R.** had agreed to the participation of the united **Germany** in **NATO.** In December 1990, Kohl was elected chancellor of the unified **Germany.**

German chancellor Helmut Kohl presided over the fall of the Berlin Wall and the reunification of East and West Germany. In 1990, he became the first leader of the reunited Germany.

In one of the many ethnic battles that rage in what was formerly Yugoslavia, the ethnic Albanian majority who live in the Kosovo region of Serbia are agitating for autonomy.

KOREA, NORTH, is a small country in Far East Asia that, by late 1992, was one of the few remaining Communist dictatorships in the world. Led by the world's oldest-serving Communist veteran, Kim-Il Sun, who became president in 1948, North Korea has slowly begun to set up ties with its much richer neighbor, South Korea. Communication links between the two countries were reestablished in late 1992 for the first time since the Korean War.

KOSOVO is a small region in southern **Serbia,** one of the six former republics of **Yugoslavia.** Most of the inhabitants are ethnic Albanians who strongly prefer a separation from **Serbia.** Since late 1988, there has been an escalating conflict between the local Albanians and Serbs, resulting in dozens of casualties.

KRAVCHUK, LEONID, is the president of **Ukraine.** The former chairman of the Supreme Soviet, Kravchuk turned nationalist after the failed coup of Soviet hard-liners in August 1991. He was elected **Ukraine'**s president in December 1991 with 62 percent of the votes, beating a well-known Ukrainian nationalist, Vyacheslav Chornovil. By 1992, Kravchuk had become one of the most visible leaders of the **Commonwealth of Independent States.**

KYRGYZSTAN, a newly independent Central Asian country, is about as large as South Dakota and has 4 million people. Known as Kirghizia in the Soviet period, the republic lies in the remote ranges of the Tien Shan mountains and is known for its sheep raising.

Rioting in June 1990 between Kirghiz and Uzbeks killed almost 200 people and injured over 1,000. Kyrgyzstan became independent after the collapse of the **U.S.S.R.** in late 1991, but immediately joined the **Commonwealth of Independent States.** Not ready for an independent existence economically or politically, Kyrgyzstan is interested in maintaining as many ties with the former Soviet republics as possible.

LANDSBERGIS, VYTAUTAS (1932–), a musicologist, became chairman of the nationalist movement of *Sajudis* in **Lithuania;** in March 1990, he was elected **Lithuania**'s president. He led the republic's successful drive for independence, but later was criticized for his authoritarianism.

LATVIA, one of the three **Baltic Republics,** lies between **Estonia** in the north and **Lithuania** in the south. It is almost the same size as West Virginia and has just 2.6 million inhabitants, of whom only 53 percent are ethnic Latvians. In May 1990, the Latvian Supreme Soviet passed a resolution declaring the republic's independence, but it took more than a year before the country shook off Soviet rule. Soon after the failed coup of hard-line apparatchiks in August 1991, Moscow recognized the independence of the three Baltic countries.

A citizenship law of 1992 granted citizenship to ethnic Latvians only. Almost half of the population, consisting mainly of ethnic Russians and Ukranians, thus became non-citizens: they cannot vote, cannot own land, and are prohibited from working in many government jobs.

LIGACHEV, YEGOR (1920–), was perhaps the most vocal opponent of **perestroika,** battling the tide of changes in the **U.S.S.R.** with great resolve but with little success. In July 1990, at the 28th Party Congress, Ligachev angrily proclaimed that "thoughtless radicalism, improvisation, and swinging from side to side have yielded us little good during the past five years." Although he received enthusiastic applause, he was defeated by a *perestroichik* candidate in an election for the deputy general secretary.

LITHUANIA, the southernmost of the three **Baltic Republics,** is slightly larger than West Virginia and has a population of 3.6 million. Medieval Lithuania embraced a much larger territory than the present republic, and often was at loggerheads with **Russia.**

Lithuania was the first Soviet republic to initiate secession from the **U.S.S.R.** The independence drive was led by the Lithuanian Restructuring Movement, better known as *Sajudis,* and its leader, musicologist **Vytautas**

Vytautas Landsbergis led the Lithuanian drive for independence as chairman of the republic's Sajudis *nationalist movement. In late 1992, the* Sajudis *party was defeated in the polls by former Communists.*

Lithuania was the first Soviet republic to initiate secession from the Soviet Union. Independence finally came in September 1991 following the failed coup by Soviet hard-liners.

Landsbergis. In March 1990, Lithuania declared its independence; in mid-April, Moscow responded by enacting an economic blockade. The conflict was eased in June when Lithuania suspended its declaration, and Moscow lifted the blockade. In January 1991, however, Soviet troops moved in to suppress the independence movement, killing over a dozen civilians.

Lithuania finally became an independent country in September 1991, after the failed coup of Soviet hard-liners. One year later, disgruntled with economic hardships and political infighting within the *Sajudis* movement, 45 percent of the Lithuanian electorate voted in parliamentary elections for reform-minded former Communists, led by Algirdas Brazauskas (who had lost against **Landsbergis** in the presidential elections in March 1990).

MACEDONIA is a name of a historic region in the Balkan peninsula that richly plays into Greek heritage; it is also the name of a former constituent republic of **Yugoslavia.** This double meaning now causes serious problems: following the example of **Slovenia, Croatia,** and **Bosnia and Herzegovina,** Macedonia proclaimed independence in 1991, but due to Greek opposition, it has not been recognized by Western nations.

MARKOVIĆ, ANTE (1924–   ), a Croatian, became prime minister of **Yugoslavia** in January 1989, and, in late December, introduced radical economic reforms. His program successfully curbed inflation, and Markovic became, for a brief period, the most respected Yugoslav leader. He seemed to be the only person capable of preserving the union, but the disintegration of the country in 1991 pushed him into oblivion.

Mircea Snegur greets crowds in August 1991, following Moldova's proclamation of independence. He was elected president of the tiny republic in December 1991.

MARXISM-LENINISM is the term for the ideological package that several generations of children and adults in the Communist countries were taught in schools and in special seminars. The main pillars of this ideology are:

- All human history until the **October Revolution** was characterized by class struggle.
- The Communist party is the vanguard of the working class.
- The **U.S.S.R.** is the cradle of socialism and the protector of all the oppressed peoples in the world.
- The imperialists, led by the **United States,** exploit workers and other oppressed peoples and support all **antisocialist, counterrevolutionary** forces in the world.
- The socialist economy is the only scientific system that has eliminated exploitation of workers.

MAZOWIECKI, TADEUSZ (1927–), a Polish Catholic intellectual active in the **Solidarity** movement, was picked by **Lech Wałęsa** in August 1989 to become prime minister of **Poland,** the first non-Communist prime minister in **Eastern Europe.** In the summer of 1990, Mazowiecki and **Wałęsa** became opponents. That fall, Mazowiecki lost his bid for the presidency and resigned.

MEČIAR, VLADIMIŔ (1943–), is prime minister of **Slovakia** and the main advocate of Slovak nationalism. A former Communist, Mečiar began to press for greater Slovak autonomy in the course of 1991 and gradually alienated a great part of the population of the **Czech Republic** by his brash style and populist demagogy. In **Slovakia,** he remains one of the most popular politicians.

MILOŠEVIĆ, SLOBODAN (1941–   ), president of **Serbia** since 1987, has been blamed for fanning the nationalist conflict in **Yugoslavia,** activities that have earned him the nickname "butcher of the Balkans." His plan of creating "Greater Serbia" has incited ethnic Serbs in **Croatia** and **Bosnia and Herzegovina** to take up arms against Croats and Muslims. In December 1992, he retained the presidency after winning 56 percent of the vote in elections monitored by Western observers.

MOLDOVA, a newly independent country and the second smallest of the former Soviet republics, is about the size of Massachusetts and Connecticut combined and has just over 4 million people. Historically part of **Romania,** Moldova was annexed to the **U.S.S.R.** in June 1940.

Ethnic Romanians represent 64 percent of the population, and the rest, mostly living in the eastern part of the country, are predominantly ethnic Russians and Ukrainians. The Moldavian language, virtually identical to Romanian, was made a state language in August 1989, which provoked opposition from the Slav minorities. In 1991, the Slavs formed a secessionist "Trans-**Dniester Republic**" on the left bank of the Dnestr. Since the start of 1992, hundreds of people have been killed in clashes between the separatists and the Moldovan security forces.

The Moldovan and Romanian governments have discussed the reunification of the two countries, although both have cautiously avoided taking any concrete steps. **Mircea Snegur,** the Moldovan president, used the phrase "two Romanias" to emphasize both this kinship and Moldovan independence.

MONGOLIA is a Central Asian country, the second nation in which Communists took power (in 1924). For the next six decades, Mongolia was a backward appendage of the **U.S.S.R.**

Mongolia's Peoples Revolutionary Party renounced **Communism** in 1990, but in two multiparty elections, in 1990 and 1992, it won over its democratic opponents. The new constitution of Mongolia pledges respect for human rights and guarantees private property.

Despite the continuing rule of former Communists, Mongolia has changed dramatically in two respects since 1990. First, the traditional religion, Buddhism, is reasserting itself with great vigor, and second, Mongolia is reclaiming its medieval hero, Genghis Khan. Genghis Khan was the leader of Mongol tribes that conquered and devastated Kievan Rus in the 13th century, and therefore his memory had to be suppressed during the Soviet-dominated period.

Even in remote Mongolia, young people have adopted many facets of Western culture—including rock music.

In early 1990, Nicaraguans ended a brief Communist interlude by voting the country's Marxist Sandinista government out of office and electing Violeta Chamorro (above) to the presidency.

NABIYEV, RAKHMAN, was the Communist boss of the Soviet republic of **Tajikistan** until 1985; he returned to power after the hard-line coup of August 1991. In May 1992, after **Tajikistan** became independent, he was forced to accept a coalition government; and in early September 1992, he was driven out of Dushanbe, **Tajikistan**'s capital. Very resilient, he and his supporters again tried to restore hard-line rule in October.

NAGORNY KARABAKH is a small region within **Azerbaijan;** three-quarters of its population is Armenian. The conflict over the enclave claimed about 1,500 people between 1988 and early 1992, by which time it had escalated into a full-scale war between **Armenia** and **Azerbaijan.** In February 1992, Armenian forces attacked the town of Khojaly and massacred its civilians.

NATO (North Atlantic Treaty Organization) was created in 1949 by a treaty between the **United States,** Canada, and 10 West European nations who agreed to join against a common enemy, Communist **U.S.S.R.** and **Eastern Europe.** Several other nations joined later, and, in 1990, the unified **Germany** also became a member. Since the enemy has now undergone a transformation, NATO plans to redefine its role.

NAZARBAYEV, NURSULTAN, a former Communist and, since late 1991, the president of independent **Kazakhstan.** He has emerged as a strong, pragmatic leader, and one of the strongest supporters of the **Commonwealth of Independent States.**

NICARAGUA is a small Central American country which briefly flirted with **Communism** in the 1980s. By that time, however, the main pillar of world **Communism,** the **U.S.S.R.,** was approaching its end and could not lend any significant support. Nicaragua's Marxist Sandinista government was voted out of office in early 1990.

NOMENCLATURE is the term designating the high party and state bureaucrats in the Communist systems who were the actual rulers of those countries. After the revolutions of late 1989, the public in Eastern European countries was shocked to see on their television screens the hidden luxuries enjoyed by nomenclature members—from golden faucets in the **Ceauşescus'** villas, to **Honecker**'s sumptuously furnished hunting lodges, to deluxe hotels exclusively for party members in **Czechoslovakia.**

OCTOBER REVOLUTION, which actually took place on November 7, 1917 (according to the old Russian calendar), in Petrograd (later Leningrad and since 1991, St. Petersburg), was one of the crucial moments of the 20th century. This was the beginning of Soviet history and of modern **Communism;** until the late 1980s, its anniversary was dutifully celebrated in all the Communist capitals. As a sad summation of the ''historical significance'' of this event, a banner was carried during the 72nd celebrations in Moscow, saying, ''Seventy Two Years of Going Nowhere.''

OSSETIA is a region in Caucasia, consisting of North Ossetia, within **Russia,** and South Ossetia, within **Georgia.** In 1991, **Georgia** stripped South Ossetia of its autonomous status, and fighting immediately erupted. The South Ossetian nationalists want to unite their region with North Ossetia. Fighting escalated in 1992, and tensions between **Russia** and **Georgia** grew. In June 1992, **Eduard Shevardnadze** of **Georgia** and **Boris Yeltsin** of **Russia** agreed to mount a joint peace-keeping operation in South Ossetia.

PANIĆ, MILAN, a Serbian-born naturalized citizen of the **United States,** was named premier of the smaller, truncated **Yugoslavia** in July 1992. He arrived in the **U.S.** in 1956, and founded the multinational drug company ICN Pharmaceuticals. As permier of **Yugoslavia,** he vowed to bring peace to his native country, but ultimately he was unable to influence events in any significant way. After losing in the presidential elections in December 1992, he resigned his post.

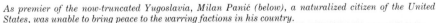

As premier of the now-truncated Yugoslavia, Milan Panić (below), a naturalized citizen of the United States, was unable to bring peace to the warring factions in his country.

PERESTROIKA, a Russian word meaning "restructuring" or "reconstruction," was introduced by **Mikhail Gorbachev** when he initiated the transformation of the Soviet economic, political, and social system. A twin term of "perestroika" was **glasnost,** an "openness" about present and past problems.

After five years, however, perestroika brought only disarray, shortages, collapse of authority, and nationalist conflict. The disintegration of the **U.S.S.R.** in late 1991 showed that efforts to transform the Soviet system were futile.

PERSONALITY CULT was a distinctive feature of Communist societies. The first and probably the greatest personality cult enveloped **Stalin,** who was elevated to a virtually godlike position and was said to be a genius in practically everything: the wisest of men, the most beloved leader, the greatest war hero, the most brilliant scientist. Streets and cities were named after Stalin, and monuments to him dotted most of the Communist world. In **Eastern Europe,** the most pronounced personality cults surrounded **Ceauşescu** of **Romania, Tito** of **Yugoslavia,** and Enver Hoxha of **Albania.**

POLAND is a flat country in central Europe, about the same size as New Mexico and with a population of 37 million. Poland's history started 1,000 years ago and, during the Middle Ages, the country was an important central European kingdom. At the end of the 18th century, the so-called "three partitions" erased Poland from the map, its territory being divided between **Russia,** Prussia, and Austria. The Polish nation survived, however, and regained its political independence in 1918.

The attack on Poland by Nazi **Germany** in September 1939 was the first act of World War II, and while German armies advanced from the west, Soviet armies entered Poland from the east. Numerous concentration camps were set up on Polish soil, the most infamous of them the extermination camp at Auschwitz.

After the war, Poland was "shifted" westward: its eastern part was retained by the **U.S.S.R.** and, in compensation, the country gained a large territory in the west, which before World War II had belonged to **Germany.** Communists took over in 1948, and, in the first period, closely followed the Soviet model. In 1956, shortly after **Nikita Khrushchev** denounced **Stalin,** Polish nationalist sentiment combined with economic grievances erupted in workers' riots in the city of Poznan. The riots brought down the Politburo and elevated Władysław Gomułka to the leadership of the party. He introduced a number of liberal reforms, abolished the farm collectivization program, and improved relations with the church. In December 1970, workers' riots in Gdansk were brutally suppressed, with at least 44 persons killed. Gomułka was replaced by Edward Gierek, who quickly became one of the main proponents of **détente** with the West. Bad economic conditions precipitated a new wave of protests in 1976.

Two years later, however, the Polish nation suddenly had a reason to rejoice when the archbishop of Cracow became Pope **John Paul II.** This event played a crucial, albeit indirect, role in the demise of **Communism** in **Eastern Europe** because it gave Poles the courage to challenge their rulers. And so, in August 1980, the famous **Solidarity** was born, and **Lech**

The Polish people retained their devotion to the Catholic Church through years of Communist rule. The church has remained a strong source of stability in post-Communist Poland.

Wałęsa became the darling of the international press. This also marked the end of Gierek's political career and the beginning of the decade of **Wojciech Jaruzelski.**

The 15 months of **Solidarity** ascendancy were a fascinating period, and it almost seemed that Communist rule was coming to an end in Poland. In December 1981, however, **Jaruzelski** declared martial law and abolished all the newly gained freedoms. Despite the ban, **Solidarity** never disappeared.

In the spring of 1989, **Solidarity** was relegalized and, in the partially free elections of June 1989, it won a resounding victory. The following August, Poland had its first non-Communist prime minister since 1948: **Tadeusz Mazowiecki,** a Catholic intellectual and a close friend and adviser of **Wałęsa.** His government concentrated on economic reform and, in early 1990, introduced radical austerity measures to curb inflation and to

Slowly but surely, private enterprise is making its mark in the former Soviet Union. Several U.S. restaurant chains have opened franchises in Moscow and other Russian cities.

set the country on a transition to a market economy. In the summer of 1990, there occurred a split within **Solidarity,** which culminated in the presidential contest between **Mazowiecki** and **Wałęsa. Wałęsa** won the presidency by a landslide in December 1990.

In the first fully free parliamentary elections in October 1991, a center-right coalition came to power, but political paralysis debilitated the country throughout 1992. A multitude of political parties and five prime ministers between October 1991 and the fall of 1992, high unemployment and inflation, and thousands of farms approaching bankruptcy were major problems. President **Wałęsa** repeatedly asked the parliament for greater powers to break the political deadlock, but was always rejected.

PRAGUE SPRING was a period in **Czechoslovakia** from early January to August 20, 1968, when, under the leadership of a reformist Communist intelligentsia, and with sometimes reluctant support from a government led by **Alexander Dubček,** the society set on a course of radical liberalization and democratization. The **U.S.S.R.,** led by **Leonid Brezhnev,** considered these changes too dangerous, and, in August, crushed the movement with the help of 500,000 **Warsaw Pact** troops. Asked in 1987 about the difference between Prague Spring and **glasnost** and **perestroika,** a Soviet Foreign Ministry spokesman replied, "nineteen years."

PRICE LIBERALIZATION has been one of the basic components of the economic transformation of former Communist countries. In a command economy, prices were fixed by the government and often remained the same for decades. The lifting of price controls was one of the first steps taken by most former Soviet republics after the collapse of the **U.S.S.R.** in December 1991, and it led to many protests and demonstrations against sudden price increases.

PRIVATIZATION of state enterprises in the former Communist countries is one of the most difficult tasks of the transition to a free-market economy. Among the various schemes tried in several countries so far, the "coupon system" introduced by **Václav Klaus** of **Czechoslovakia** seems to works best. It consists of transforming state enterprises into share-holding companies, with individual shares being distributed among the population. Other ways to privatize include selling companies to domestic and foreign investors, or distributing shares among employees of each enterprise. Privatization of land in **Eastern Europe** is much easier: in most cases it is simply returned to its original owners. In the former Soviet Union, however, land privatization after seven decades of **Communism** is only in the earliest stages.

REAGAN, RONALD (1911–   ), 40th president of the **United States,** from 1981 to 1989. He was elected less than a year after the Soviet invasion of **Afghanistan** and, in his first presidential term, called the **U.S.S.R.** "an evil empire." He accelerated the arms race, thus putting additional pressure on the **U.S.S.R.** and indirectly contributing to the deepening crisis of the Soviet system. Two months after Reagan's second inauguration, **Mikhail Gorbachev** became the leader of the **U.S.S.R.,** and, in the fall of 1986, the two leaders met in the first of their four summit meetings.

REFUGEES. One of the most serious problems since the end of the **Cold War** has been the massive displacement of peoples. The worst case is in **Yugoslavia,** where the civil war uprooted about 2.3 million persons by late 1992. Of the 500,000 who left the country, **Germany** accepted about 200,000 people, **Hungary** 60,000, and Sweden 41,000.

    Germany has traditionally had the most liberal laws on refugees, but this influx has caused domestic problems, including rioting in many

During a summit meeting in May and June 1988, U.S. President Ronald Reagan and Soviet leader Mikhail Gorbachev made a historic stroll through Moscow's Red Square.

cities. In all of 1991, 256,000 asylum seekers entered **Germany;** in just the first eight months of 1992, more than 274,000 people applied for asylum. The number of asylum seekers entering **Germany** in 1992 is expected to reach 500,000.

RESTITUTIONS AND COMPENSATIONS are important components of the transformation of former Communist systems, particularly in **Eastern Europe.** Unfortunately, these efforts to rectify damages caused by the previous regime have in turn led to new problems. What should be the cut-off date to consider returning confiscated property? When the Communists took over, in the late 1940s? Or just after the war? Or should one start with the confiscations by Nazis? And how should victims of **Communism** and their descendants be compensated for loss of lives, terms in prison, loss of jobs? How can monetary compensations be calculated? Will not the restitutions and compensations lead to new injustices?

REVISIONISM is a term that used to be applied by hard-line Communists to various types of reform-minded Communists. In 1948, **Tito**'s **Yugoslavia** was branded revisionist and expelled from the Cominform, an international body of Communist countries led by the **U.S.S.R.**; when **Nikita Khrushchev** denounced **Stalin, Albania** accused the **U.S.S.R.** of revisionism. In the 1970s and 1980s, the word was largely replaced by the expression **antisocialist.**

ROMAN, PETRE, prime minister of **Romania** from June 1990 until September 1991, presided over a youthful technocratic cabinet that initiated economic reforms, including **price liberalization** and voucher **privatization.** In March 1992, Roman was confirmed as the president of the National Salvation Front, the group that has ruled **Romania** since the overthrow of the Communist regime.

ROMANI (GYPSIES) are one of the most visible European minorities. Originally from northern India, groups of wandering Gypsies came to Europe in the 14th century and spread throughout the continent. During World War II, Nazi **Germany** conducted genocide against Gypsies, murdering about 500,000 of them in concentration camps.

As prime minister of Romania, Petre Roman (right) has presided over the country's economic liberalization.

Unlike the rather peaceful government changes elsewhere in Eastern Europe, Romania's overthrow of Communism in 1989 was accompanied by much death and destruction.

It is not known precisely how many Romani live in **Eastern Europe,** but the numbers certainly reach several million. Increasing criminality in the post-Communist period has often involved Romani, and this has in turn provoked right-wing attacks on them by skinheads and various neo-Nazi groups.

ROMANIA is a country in the Balkans, bordering on the Black Sea, slightly larger than Utah, and with 23 million people. It is the easternmost outpost of a Romance language: Romanian derives from Latin as was spoken in the eastern part of the Roman Empire. Vlado Tepes the Impaler, a medieval Romanian hero who fought the Turks, was popularized in a 19th-century novel and turned into the modern Dracula.

Long under the rule of foreign powers, present-day Romania began to emerge in the middle of the 19th century. Between the world wars, it was a royal dictatorship, and then it fought on the side of the Germans. In 1944, the Communists took over and, for the next two decades, Romania closely followed the Soviet model.

A new period began in 1965, when **Nicolae Ceauşescu** was elevated to the leadership of Romania. The **Ceauşescu** era was first marked by a more independent foreign policy and an opening to the West. In the 1980s, in order to reach his goal of paying off all foreign debt, **Ceauşescu** wreaked untold hardships upon the people. Drastic cuts in energy darkened Romanian apartments and streets, and in winter there was not enough heat. Food was exported, and the people were half-starving. To compound the general bleakness of life, the government introduced the so-called "systematization plan," which called for the demolition of up to 7,000 villages and the transfer of their inhabitants into huge agro-industrial complexes. Amid the suffering **Ceauşescu** embarked on grandiose public-works projects.

The end of the **Ceauşescu** era was a combination of a popular revolt and a coup. It started on December 17, 1989, in the predominantly Hungarian city of Timisoara, when the Securitate police and army troops fired into a demonstration. Protests then spread to other parts of the country and, on December 21, fighting broke out in the capital. The army took a stand against **Ceauşescu;** he fled with his wife, but both were captured and executed on December 25, 1989. The National Salvation Front (NSF), consisting mostly of former high Communist officials and led by **Ion Iliescu,** emerged as the leading political group and gained popular support by abolishing some of the most hated decrees of the **Ceauşescu** era.

Unfortunately, the violence did not end with the overthrow of the dictator. Violent confrontations occurred several times during 1990, between pro-government miners and anti-NSF demonstrators and between Romanian peasants and the Hungarian minority in Transylvania. In May 1990, the first free Romanian elections since 1937 took place, with 82 registered political parties. The major ones, apart from the NSF, were led by exiles, and most were immature and badly organized. The extreme repression under **Ceauşescu** (when even typewriters had to be registered) prevented the rise of a strong intellectual middle class that would have been the natural starting point for new political parties. It was therefore no surprise that the NSF won an overwhelming victory.

Throughout 1991, demonstrations, strikes, and anti-government protests continued, but at the same time the parliament approved a new constitution, in November 1991, defining Romania as a state committed to pluralism, human rights, and a market economy. In late 1992, the country was still beset by huge problems, but it was beginning to resemble a functioning democracy.

RUSSIA was the largest of the Soviet constituent republics, stretching from **Eastern Europe** to the Pacific. It is almost as large as the whole of South America, and it has a population of 144 million. **Boris Yeltsin,** president of Russia since May 1990, led the opposition to the hard-line coup in August 1991 and then presided over the final demise of the **U.S.S.R.** and the establishment of the **Commonwealth of Independent States.**

In mid-1992, nearly half of the population of Russia was below the official poverty line, but there were enough signs of positive changes to make it possible for optimists to believe that the country will manage its transition from **Communism** to democracy without major bloodshed.

SAKHAROV, ANDREI (1921–89), the father of the Soviet H-bomb, became in 1953 the youngest member of the Soviet Academy of Sciences. In the early 1960s, he began to challenge Soviet authorities, and his human-rights activities earned him the Nobel Peace Prize in 1975.

After Sakharov sharply criticized the Soviet invasion of **Afghanistan** in December 1979, he was exiled to the town of Gorki in January 1980. He did not remain silent, although his communication with the outside world became ever more difficult. One day in December 1986, a telephone was suddenly installed in Sakharov's apartment in Gorki, and the next day a personal call from **Mikhail Gorbachev** summoned the exiled dissident to Moscow. It was an event without precedent in Soviet history. In April 1989, Sakharov was elected to the Congress of People's Deputies, but he died of a heart attack in December.

Sarajevo, the capital of Bosnia and Herzegovina, has been the scene of nearly constant bombardment by Serbian guerrilla forces. Thousands of people have died or become refugees.

SARAJEVO, the capital of **Bosnia and Herzegovina** in former **Yugoslavia,** has come to personify the ethnic cruelty of the post-Communist world. Besieged by Serbian guerrilla forces on the surrounding hills, the city that became known to the younger generation during the Winter Olympic Games of 1984 was being systematically destroyed by bombardment and sniper fire. United Nations peacekeepers took charge of the airport at the end of June 1992 and started delivering food and medicine.

SERBIA was the largest of the six republics comprising the pre-1992 **Yugoslavia.** Serbs are a Slavic people who for centuries had been under Ottoman rule; they are predominantly Orthodox Christians, and their language is written in the Cyrillic script.

In 1987, when a hard-line nationalist, **Slobodan Milošević,** became the leader of the Communist Party, Serbia set out on a path of ethnic conflict with the other nationalities of **Yugoslavia.** The first clashes took place in the province of **Kosovo,** but they have been since overshadowed by the brutal war in **Croatia** in 1991 and the senseless slaughter in **Bosnia and Herzegovina** in 1992.

SHEVARDNADZE, EDUARD (1928–   ), a native of **Georgia,** became known throughout the world as **Mikhail Gorbachev**'s foreign minister from 1985 to 1990. In December 1990, he resigned in protest against the "approaching dictatorship," but he briefly resumed his post after the August 1991 attempted coup by Soviet hard-liners. In March 1992, Shevardnadze returned to his native country and became chairman of **Georgia**'s provisional State Council. In October 1992, he was elected by 90 percent of the voters to the post of Speaker of the Parliament.

East Germany carried out a "shoot-to-kill" policy on any person trying to escape into West Germany. More than 200 persons were killed while trying to flee to the West.

"SHOOT-TO-KILL" was the policy of the government of **East Germany,** which ordered border guards to kill anyone trying to cross into West Germany. According to 1992 estimates, more than 200 East Germans were killed in these attempts. **Erich Honecker,** the former East German leader, was charged with manslaughter in connection with this policy, and several former East German border guards were sentenced to prison terms.

SINATRA DOCTRINE. On October 25, 1989, Soviet Foreign Ministry spokesman Gennady Gerasimov said on American television that the new **Warsaw Pact** doctrine could now be called the "Sinatra Doctrine," after the famous Frank Sinatra song "I Did It My Way." From now on, Gerasimov implied, all countries in the pact can "do it their way," without fear of Soviet military intervention. The Sinatra Doctrine replaced the much more ominous **Brezhnev Doctrine,** which threatened military intervention in any **Warsaw Pact** country that strayed from the Soviet fold.

SLOVAKIA was the eastern half of **Czechoslovakia;** since January 1993, it has been an independent country. About the size of New Hampshire and Vermont combined, it is a mostly mountainous region inhabited by 5 million people. For 1,000 years, Slovakia was part of **Hungary.** Its only period of political independence came during World War II, when it became a puppet Nazi state. After the war, it again became part of **Czechoslovakia.**

Slovaks' yearning for an independent national identity became personified in a populist politician **Vladimír Mečiar,** who during 1991 and 1992 got into a deepening conflict with Czech politicians; in late 1992, he led Slovakia to independence. The sovereignty declaration by the Slovak National Council in July 1992 proclaimed that "the thousand years' striving of the Slovak nation for self-realization has been accomplished." Slovakia became an independent country on January 1, 1993.

SLOVENIA, one of the six constituent republics of pre-1992 **Yugoslavia** and, since June 1991, an independent country, lies in the north of the Balkan peninsula, bordering on Austria. It is about the size of New Jersey and its population is just under 2 million. Since there were no Serbs living within Slovenia, the republic escaped the violence that erupted in **Croatia** in 1991 and in **Bosnia and Herzegovina** in 1992. It was the richest and the most Westernized of all the Yugoslav republics.

SNEGUR, MIRCEA, a former Communist turned nationalist, was elected president of the former Soviet republic of **Moldova** in December 1991. During the August 1991 coup by Soviet hard-liners, Snegur banned all Communist Party activity.

SOCIALISM, a word that dates from the early 19th century, has been one of the most abused and misused political terms of the 20th century. It has many meanings: when **Stalin** built his "socialism in one country," the system he had in mind was a society totally controlled by him, with much emphasis on heavy industry, forced labor by prisoners, and merciless struggle against the "class enemy." **Alexander Dubček**'s "socialism with a human face" was a much more benevolent system, in which the Communist Party would still rule, but in consultation with other groups in society. **Dubček**'s vision led to **Czechoslovakia**'s brief **Prague Spring** in 1968. Yet another kind is the socialism of western social democratic parties, which advocate the modern day "welfare state."

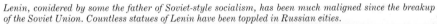

Lenin, conidered by some the father of Soviet-style socialism, has been much maligned since the breakup of the Soviet Union. Countless statues of Lenin have been toppled in Russian cities.

In 1981, the independent trade union Solidarity emerged in the shipbuilding city of Gdansk, Poland. In a matter of months, Solidarity had a membership of over 10 million.

SOLIDARITY, an independent trade union in **Poland,** was the major protagonist in the last decade of Eastern European **Communism.** On August 14, 1981, an unemployed electrician named **Lech Wałęsa** began to lead a 17-day occupation strike that resulted in the formation of the Solidarity trade union. The union soon claimed a membership of 10 million. During the next 15 months, it rapidly evolved into a powerful organization that began to demand free elections and a referendum on forming a legitimate non-Communist government. On December 13, 1981, under pressure from the **U.S.S.R.** (still firmly ruled by **Leonid Brezhnev**), Polish Prime Minister **Wojciech Jaruzelski** declared martial law, suspended Solidarity, and arrested its leaders and activists—more than 10,000 people altogether.

But this was just one lost battle: with the absence of Soviet pressure after **Mikhail Gorbachev** came to power, Solidarity began to reassert itself. In 1989, it was relegalized and participated in the partially free elections for the Polish parliament, winning virtually all available seats.

Once the Communist adversary was gone, Solidarity split and in 1990 divided into two broad factions: the right-leaning Center Agreement, led by **Wałęsa**; and the left-leaning Citizens' Movement for Democratic Action, associated with urban intellectuals.

SOLZHENITSYN, ALEKSANDR (1918–   ), a leading Soviet **dissident** and a winner of the Nobel Prize for Literature in 1970. He was forcibly exiled from the **U.S.S.R.** in early 1974 after he published his *Gulag Archipelago,* considered one of the most important books of the 20th century for its vivid revelation of the horrors of the system of prisons and forced labor camps established under **Stalin.**

Solzhenitsyn settled in Vermont and concentrated on writing his mammoth historical reevaluation of Soviet history. His Soviet citizenship was restored in August 1990 and, in 1992, he announced his decision to return to **Russia.**

STALIN, JOSEPH (1879–1953), shaped the Soviet system in many ways: he made the **U.S.S.R.** a world superpower and he greatly contributed to the defeat of Hitler. At the same time, he inflicted on the Soviet people extreme suffering. No one killed as many Communists as he did: during the height of his terror, in the 1930s, it was much safer for a Communist to live in a Western country than in the **U.S.S.R.**

Stalin, although Georgian by birth, was a product of Russian history. The system created by him caused so much damage not only because it was brutal and intolerant, but also because it systematically rewarded the worst human qualities—subservience, lying, lack of initiative, servility, and envy—and punished such qualities as courage, creativity, industriousness, and truthfulness.

Much more devious than Hitler, Stalin duped quite a few Westerners who praised his simplicity and even charm. The **personality cult** elevated him to a godlike position. Despite several decades of **de-Stalinization,** it was only in the late 1980s that the Soviet people began to learn that their beloved leader was actually responsible for some 30 to 50 million deaths.

TAJIKISTAN, a Central Asian republic about the size of Wisconsin, has 4.6 million people; until 1991, it was part of the **U.S.S.R.** The Tajiks are a Persian-speaking people who even during the Soviet era continued to live in very traditional ways.

From the time of the hard-line coup of August 1991, Tajikistan has been a battleground, with Communist and opposition forces (the latter

Joseph Stalin (left, in 1945 with U.S. President Harry Truman and British Prime Minister Winston Churchill) gave Soviet Communism its authoritarian nature.

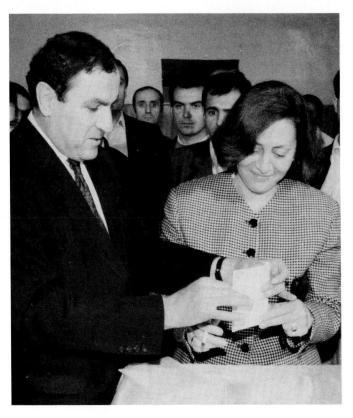

Levon Ter-Petrosyan (left, with his wife Ludmila) has managed to hold on to the presidency of Armenia despite setbacks in the continuing war with Azerbaijan.

consisting of anti-Communists and Islamic fundamentalists) repeatedly locked in armed conflict. The supporters of **Rakhman Nabiyev,** a former Communist who tried to hold tenaciously to power, have battled Islamic groupings, and the civil war claimed over 2,000 casualties in the course of 1992.

TER-PETROSYAN, LEVON, president of **Armenia,** was blamed for setbacks in the war with **Azerbaijan** and had to face a no-confidence vote in parliament in August 1992. He survived the vote and then appealed to the **Commonwealth of Independent States** to assist **Armenia** against Azerbaijani aggression.

TITO, JOSIP BROZ (1892–1980), born in **Croatia,** was the powerful postwar leader of **Yugoslavia.** He led the Communist guerrillas during World War II, and then remained the paramount chief of the country until his death. Although Tito was an authoritarian ruler, he was not the diabolical dictator as was **Stalin** or **Ceauşescu.** He held the country together, balancing traditional national animosities and making **Yugoslavia** a special case of a relatively liberal socialist country.

TUDJMAN, FRANJO, head of the right-of-center Croatian Democratic Union, was first elected president of **Croatia** in 1990. He was reelected for his second term in August 1992.

TURKMENISTAN is a newly independent Central Asian republic about the size of Nevada and Utah combined; it has about 4 million inhabitants. The new statehood has largely resulted in economic problems and uncertainties.

UKRAINE was the second largest constituent republic of the **U.S.S.R.,** twice the size of Arizona and with 50 million people. Centering around the ancient city of Kiev, Ukrainians have had a love-hate relationship with Russians for centuries.

Ukraine became independent in late 1991 and joined the **Commonwealth of Independent States.** One of the first problems that the leaders of the newly independent Ukraine had to grapple with was the control of the Black Sea naval fleet stationed in Sevastopol, a port in the **Crimea.** In August 1992, **Russia** and Ukraine agreed to keep the fleet under joint control for three years, after which the fleet would be divided between the two countries. Ukraine has also been reluctant to give up the nuclear weapons in its possession. Under the leadership of **Leonid Kravchuk,** a Communist-turned-nationalist, the new country is grappling with severe economic problems—as are all the other former Soviet republics.

UNION OF SOVIET SOCIALIST REPUBLICS (the **U.S.S.R.** or the Soviet Union), was for most of the 20th century the largest country in the world, almost 2.5 times the size of the **United States,** stretching from central Europe to the Pacific across 11 time zones; it had more than 100 nationalities and 112 officially recognized languages. A country of contrasts, its social and political settings ranged from **Lithuania,** a very Westernized Baltic country in the West, to the Chukchi Siberian groups in the northeast, whose lives resemble those of the Canadian Eskimo, and to the Muslim republics in Central Asia.

The U.S.S.R. was the heir to the Russian Empire, which had emerged in the 13th century as the little landlocked duchy of Muscovy, and then gradually expanded to roughly its present size. **Russia** traditionally had a complex relationship with Europe, trying during successive periods to emulate European civilization, and yet resisting Western ways. When the Bolsheviks took over in 1917, in the **October Revolution,** and emerged victorious after three years of civil war, they believed that they started a "world revolu-

Russians jubilantly celebrated in the streets following the failure of the August 1991 coup attempt by Soviet hardliners. The coup attempt ultimately led to the collapse of the Soviet Union.

tion." Instead, their "social experiment" became one of the two greatest tragedies, together with Nazism, of the 20th century.

The Soviet Union went through several periods: from the early revolutionary euphoria, to **Stalin**'s terror of the 1930s, to a great patriotic upsurge during World War II, and then to the postwar period of empire building, **Khrushchev**'s **de-Stalinization, Brezhnev**'s **détente,** and finally the period of "stagnation" of the 1980s. By then, it was becoming increasingly obvious that the system did not work: the U.S.S.R. was a world superpower, with a great arsenal of nuclear weapons and space technology, and yet the average villagers lived almost as they did in the 19th century. In the cities, the time spent standing in lines for everyday items represented millions of lost hours of work and instilled the people with an overwhelming resentment and dissatisfaction. Nothing seemed to work, and no one seemed to believe in anything anymore; the teachings of **Marxism-Leninism** were just empty formulas repeated automatically when it was required. Alcoholism became a major problem as both men and women resorted to the ubiquitous Russian vodka to drown their sorrows.

When **Mikhail Gorbachev** embarked on his reform course in 1985, he opened a Pandora's box. His **glasnost** and **perestroika** shook the stagnant waters of the system, and at first promised to be the miraculous medicine needed to put the society back into shape. It turned out, however, that the patient was even sicker than it seemed, and while **Gorbachev** was reaping applause throughout the Western world, his own country was getting into deeper and deeper difficulties: growing economic problems, shortages of everything, nationalist conflicts, separatism, and loss of political authority.

By the end of 1990, a mood of national exasperation had taken hold of the country. **Gorbachev** responded by first allying himself with hardliners, which prompted the resignation of **Eduard Shevardnadze** in December 1990 and led to the violent crackdown in the **Baltic Republics** in January 1991. In April 1991, **Gorbachev** changed his mind and concluded an agreement with nine Soviet leaders about a new union treaty, which was supposed to give individual republics much greater independence from Moscow. This in turn provoked fears in the "old-guard" and culminated in the botched coup of August 1991. After that the fate of the Soviet Union was sealed: four more months of political and social upheaval ended with the final demise of the Communist colossus on December 25, 1991.

UNITED STATES has fascinated the peoples in the **U.S.S.R.** and in **Eastern Europe** for decades. Despite being violently and continually attacked by official propaganda, it has been admired as a country of jeans, rock and roll, and tall, smiling people with beautiful white teeth. Several generations of Eastern European children have been brought up on adventure books by Karl May, a German who never set foot in America, but wrote a series of novels about the American Indians. The U.S. has also been known from the movies and from the works of such extremely popular authors as Ernest Hemingway and Kurt Vonnegut. Even now, with many more personal contacts and the **Cold War** rhetoric gone, the U.S. continues to be a somewhat frightening, mysterious, inscrutable, and tremendously attractive place.

Vietnam was united as a Communist country in 1975 after a prolonged war involving the U.S. Many groups are still searching for evidence of Americans left behind after the U.S. withdrew its forces.

UZBEKISTAN, twice as large as Utah, is a Central Asian Soviet republic with over 18 million people. The country has a colorful history: in the 14th century, the city of Samarkand was the capital of the sophisticated empire of Timurlane. In the late 1980s, during the heyday of **glasnost,** a number of high Uzbek officials were sentenced for taking bribes and for corruption.

Uzbekistan's president in early 1992 declared that the newly independent country would follow the "Turkish model," that is, a combination of a free-market economy with moderate Islam.

VIETNAM is a Southeast Asian Communist country that was for 16 years, from the late 1950s until 1975, involved in a war with the **United States.** The fall of **Communism** in the **U.S.S.R.,** the main supporter of Vietnam during that war, has led to gradual political and economic liberalization and to improved ties with the **United States.** These ties were further strengthened by Vietnam's recent cooperation regarding the fate of Americans still listed as missing-in-action from the Vietnam War.

VUKOVAR, a city in easternmost **Croatia,** became a ghost town in late 1991 when it was almost totally demolished in the war between Croats and Serbs. Most of its 45,000 inhabitants were either killed or fled.

WAŁĘSA, LECH (1943–), a high-school-educated electrician, was the leader of **Solidarity** in 1980–81 and the Nobel Peace Prize winner in 1983. His political activism began during the December 1970 strikes in Gdansk; by August 1980, he had become an international celebrity almost overnight. In 1987, he published his autobiography, *A Way of Hope.* On December 9, 1990, Wałęsa, in a landslide victory, was elected president of **Poland,** but because of continuing economic problems and political instability, his popularity had dropped significantly by 1992.

WARSAW PACT was the name of a military alliance formed in 1955 in response to **NATO.** Its original members were **Albania, Bulgaria, Czechoslovakia, East Germany, Hungary, Poland, Romania,** and the **U.S.S.R.;** Albania stopped participating in the alliance in the early 1960s, and formally left in 1968. The only military action that the Warsaw Pact armies ever took was the invasion of **Czechoslovakia** in August 1968; **Romania** did not participate. The Warsaw Pact was formally dissolved in July 1991.

YELTSIN, BORIS (1931–   ), president of **Russia** since 1990, is the foremost leader in the post-Communist world. His career in the late 1980s provided vivid proof of how things had changed in the **U.S.S.R.** In the fall of 1987, Yeltsin was attacked by **Mikhail Gorbachev** and sacked from the Moscow municipal committee. If **Stalin** had taken a dislike to him, Yeltsin would have paid with his life; under **Brezhnev,** he would have become a "nonperson" (like **Khrushchev**). But under **Gorbachev,** Yeltsin made a spectacular comeback in the spring of 1989, when, in a landslide victory, he was elected to the Congress of People's Deputies.

In June 1990, Yeltsin was elected President of **Russia** and the following month, at the 28th Party Congress, he dramatically quit the Communist Party. By the fall of 1990, Yeltsin had become vastly more popular than **Gorbachev,** and in August 1991, he courageously led the opposition to the attempted coup by Soviet hard-liners. Yeltsin has by late 1992 gained recognition for his constructive handling of the vast problems of post-Communist **Russia.**

YUGOSLAVIA is now a name for two political entities. From 1929 until 1992, with an interruption during World War II, it was a name for the country of South Slavs, which was popularly described as *one country* with *two alphabets* (Latin and Cyrillic), *three religions* (Catholicism, Eastern Orthodoxy, and Islam), *four languages* (Serbo-Croatian, Slovenian, Macedonian, and Albanian), *five nationalities* (Serbs, Croats, Slovenians, Macedonians, and Albanians), and *six constituent republics* (**Serbia, Croatia, Slovenia, Bosnia and Herzegovina, Macedonia,** and Montenegro).

This mosaic burst apart in the early 1990s. In April 1992, a new, truncated Yugoslavia was proclaimed, consisting only of **Serbia** and Montenegro. It is about half the size of the previous Yugoslavia, with about half of the population.

During World War II, **Yugoslavia** was the scene of a fierce guerrilla war between partisans and groups allied with the Fascists; some 1.7 million Yugoslavs were killed. The fighting left deep scars and lingering animosities, especially between the Serbs and the Croats. After the war, the charismatic Communist leader **Josip Broz Tito** held the country firmly together until his death in 1980. Under **Tito,** Yugoslavia balanced on the dividing line between a typical Communist state (it had only one party, with supreme powers; there was press censorship; and people were put in prison for political reasons) and an open liberal society.

When **Tito** died, the buried nationalist passions slowly reemerged and then erupted in a fury. Even before **Croatia** declared independence, violent conflicts between the Serbian population in **Croatia** and Croats foreshadowed the brutal confrontation of 1991. In early 1992, the country had a brief respite, with a cease-fire in **Croatia** and deployment of U.N. peacekeeping forces. In March, however, **Bosnia and Herzegovina** de-

In August 1991, Boris Yeltsin courageously led the opposition to the attemped coup by Soviet hard-liners. As Russia's president, he has had to deal with the dismantling of the vast Communist system.

clared independence and an even more ferocious war began. According to a United Nations report of the summer of 1992, civil war in Yugoslavia displaced 2.3 million people, of which 1.8 million remained within the region and 500,000 left for other countries.

The Belgrade leadership of the new Yugoslavia claims that the war in **Bosnia and Herzegovina** is waged by Bosnian Serbs, but there is clear evidence that they are supported, both militarily and ideologically, by **Serbia**. On September 22, 1992, the new Yugoslavia was expelled from the United Nations, the first time any sitting member was ejected.

ZHELEV, ZHELYU (1935–   ), the president of **Bulgaria** since August 1990, was one of the very few Bulgarian **dissidents** during the country's Communist era. In 1965, he was expelled from the Communist Party as the result of an essay he wrote that questioned the basis of Lenin's philosophical theories. Zhelev won re-election to a second presidential term in January 1992.

ZHIVKOV, TODOR (1911–   ). Leader of the Communist Party in **Bulgaria** from 1954 until his removal in November 1989, Zhivkov had the second-longest tenure among the East European leaders, after the Albanian Enver Hoxha. In September 1992, Zhivkov was convicted of embezzling state funds and sentenced to seven years in prison. He was the first Communist leader to be tried in an open trial—the Romanian **Nicolae Ceauşescu** was executed after a closed military trial, and **Erich Honecker** of former **East Germany** was awaiting trial in late 1992.

Ethnic unrest has swept through many of the regions long controlled by Communist governments.

Looking Toward the Next Century

The ease with which the Communist regimes were toppled in most Eastern European countries created the illusion that open, democratic societies could rise virtually overnight from the ashes of Communist dictatorship. But democracy is not the only alternative to Communism: as multiethnic Yugoslavia and Caucasia tragically demonstrate, the end of one-party rule can also lead to the reemergence of historical nationalist hatreds and violence. Furthermore, democracy has always been the result of a long maturing process; even those post-Communist countries without ethnic strife are undergoing painful labor pains. The results will most likely be uneven: some democratic governments now in their infancy will mature into healthier and stronger institutions than will others.

Challenges of Post-Communism

Ethnic and political violence.   Yugoslavia represents the most visible case, yet the conflicts in Transcaucasia and elsewhere in the former Soviet Union are no less ferocious. The fighting results mostly from historic hatreds. The Communist dictatorships often exacerbated these animosities by arbitrarily drawing geographic borders with little or no regard to ethnic and historic claims. Stalin in particular was well aware of the old dictum "divide and rule." The small republic of Moldova, the scene of much ethnic fighting, is a typical example of such artificial borders: the secessionist "Dnestr Republic" was not a part of the historic Moldavia; rather, it was added to Moldavia by Stalin after the Soviet Union took the region from Romania in 1940.

In Central Asia, the violent conflict that has convulsed Tajikistan has a more political nature. The forces of the Communist old-guard are led by the former president, Rakhman Nabiyev; their adversaries include various democratic and Islamic groups. It is likely, however, that even in Tajikistan, ethnic factors are playing into the conflict.

There is yet another violence, now ominously present in Germany. Ethnic fighting and economic hardships on the one hand and open borders on the other have led to a great displacement of people. Indeed, all Central European countries now have refugees in their midst. Germany, with its liberal immigration policy, has attracted hundreds of thousands of people from the East. This influx is now proving a nightmare, as groups of young German rightists and neo-Nazis mount a hate campaign against the immigrants. Such violence is not, of course, peculiar to Germany. Attacks on Gypsies, Vietnamese, and other foreigners have also taken place in Czechoslovakia, Hungary, and Poland. Many of the young people involved in these actions are unemployed and blame the refugees for their economic difficulties.

Criminality. In all post-Communist societies, the less-regimented atmosphere and the disappearance of many previous controls have led to a rise in criminal behavior. Throughout what was once the Communist world, there are now gangs dealing in drugs, smuggling refugees, and engaging in various swindling schemes, robberies, muggings, and murders. The police, who for years terrorized the population, are only slowly being transformed into a protective force.

Economic transformation from a command economy to a free-market system is made more difficult by the worldwide recession. But even if generous aid were forthcoming from the West, this economic transformation would be a tremendous task. The chances of successfully introducing a new economic system depend largely on the economic health and legacy of each country before Communism was introduced.

The pillars of the economic transformation are price liberalization and privatization of state enterprises and land, which should ultimately lead to increased productivity, greater efficiency, and higher-quality

Many citizens of the formerly Communist countries have fled their economically distressed lands for the more prosperous Western European nations, creating a severe refugee problem.

Long-suppressed bigotries quickly resurfaced in the newly liberalized Eastern European societies. In some places, groups of neo-Nazis and skinheads have terrorized the immigrant population.

products, but there are many other components as well. All the post-Communist governments must create modern banking systems and stock exchanges, develop new tax systems, and adopt clear legislation about unemployment benefits, bankruptcies, and foreign investments. The degree of economic hardship varies from the relatively painless process in the Czech Republic (which has sailed through the first years of its economic transformation with little unemployment and very manageable inflation) to the total economic collapse in Albania and the overwhelming shortages occurring throughout much of the former Soviet Union.

Political transformation.   To eliminate the top leadership of the Communist pyramid was relatively easy; unfortunately, to eliminate the influence of the Communist "old-boys' network" at the lower levels is proving to be much more difficult. The *nomenclature* was a sort of private club, somewhat similar to the members of the British public school system—ministers, factory directors, heads of state and party agencies. All those who held the actual power knew each other, they socialized and spent vacations in the same privileged spots, their children played together, and they spoke the same language. After decades in power, few of them are willing to step aside. Rather, they may have changed coats and suddenly become democrats, entrepreneurs, or nationalists.

Meanwhile, the newly emerging political parties are squabbling among themselves, producing an excess of political fragmentation, infighting, and pettiness. The art of civilized political discourse is still largely absent.

Educating new leaders.   Radical economic and political change requires strong leaders. Such leaders are only now being trained in new schools and educational centers throughout Eastern Europe. A busy exchange of professional and educational visits with the West is underway —both by Westerners coming to the former Communist countries and by citizens of those countries going to the West. These exchanges have produced fascinating encounters between two worlds that were divided for such a long time.

Fixing the environment is a tremendous challenge for the simple reason that so many places in the former Communist world are ecological disasters. For years, people in those countries knew that they were living in an unhealthy environment, but the truth about the ecological damage turned out to be much harsher than most suspected. Life expectancy has dropped in Eastern Europe and the former Soviet Union partly because of the high level of air pollution and the widespread chemical contamination of food. Among the most affected areas are the coal belt in southeastern Germany, southern Poland, and northern Czech Republic; northern Transylvania, in Romania; and the whole area east of the Aral Sea, in Central Asia.

Facing the past is a very painful problem: how should you punish those who caused harm and compensate those who suffered, without causing new injustices and new suffering? The East German secret police, *Stasi,* had 85,000 full-time agents and over 500,000 part-time informers: should all of them somehow pay for their activities, for instance, by having their names published? A published list of people who collaborated with the secret police in Czechoslovakia provoked much criticism because it included the names of many innocent people and excluded the names of those who directed and organized the spying.

Only a handful of former Communist leaders have been punished; Romania's Nicolae Ceauşescu, and his wife Elena, were the only ones who paid with their lives. The plotters of the failed Soviet coup were arrested; Bulgaria's Todor Zhivkov was sentenced to several years in prison; in November 1992, former East German leader Erich Honecker was being tried; and some minor officials were tried, convicted, and sentenced to short prison terms in Romania, Bulgaria, and Czechoslovakia. In the former Soviet Union, the Communist party was suspended after the coup, but in Eastern Europe most Communist parties have changed names and are still busily involved in politics.

The world was shocked to discover the catastrophic condition of the environment in the formerly Communist countries. In Eastern Europe, the situation could take decades to remedy.

Slowly but surely, private enterprise is making headway in the former Soviet Union. Many little shops have opened but, unfortunately, few people have the money to purchase anything but necessities.

It is interesting to note that many of today's most ardent nationalist leaders, including the notorious Slobodan Milosević of Serbia, Mircea Snegur of Moldova, and Vladimír Mečiar of Slovakia, are former Communist leaders.

Another problem concerns expropriations of property by Communists. In Eastern Europe, where the Communist regimes lasted less than 50 years, it is still possible to locate the original owners of many small businesses and real estate. In various schemes differing from country to country, the original owners or their families are either regaining their properties or are being compensated for their loss. Unfortunately, the paperwork alone for this process is overwhelming.

Social and cultural change will probably require at least one generation in Eastern Europe and, most likely, even more time in the former Soviet Union. After decades of living in a morally corrupt world, one in which lying, stealing, and hypocrisy were a way of life, it is extremely difficult to learn new ways. There is a continuing distrust in politicians. Everywhere in the former Soviet Union, there exists a pervasive feeling that anyone engaged in private enterprise is making an unfair profit. Perhaps worst of all, there is a great deal of envy. The very few enterprising private farmers in Russia complain about the hostility they perceive from their neighbors for being successful. Similar complaints are heard from hundreds of other capable and talented individuals in the former Communist world.

People in Communist societies had grown accustomed to being taken care of by the state. Indeed, the state directed virtually every aspect of life, from education to employment to housing. One aspect of this dependence on the state was that no one felt truly responsible for his or her own life. The state was blamed for all difficulties. Many people, particularly the older generation, still persist in this attitude—someone else is responsible for their problems.

The Regional Outlook

Central Europe. The central European countries—Poland, former East Germany, the newly independent Czech and Slovak republics, and Hungary—will likely enter the 21st century as stable pluralist societies, but they still have hard times ahead of them.

Balkan countries. Among the Balkan countries, Bulgaria and Albania are slowly discarding their Communist past and forging ahead. Romania is still ruled by former Communists, but it has embarked on economic transformation and its human rights record is improving.

The former Yugoslavia. When Josip Broz Tito was still the Yugoslav leader, warnings were occasionally heard that Yugoslavia would not survive his death—and yet it seemed such a peaceful, pleasant country. All this now seems like ages ago as the former "land of south Slavs" is disappearing in gunsmoke. The fighting will leave terrible scars and hatreds for years to come.

Russia. The core of the former Soviet Union, mighty Russia (still the largest country in the world) has a very long road ahead of it. Creating a stable democratic regime will be difficult; fortunately, there are enough signs to indicate that this goal is possible.

Ukraine and Belarus. Russia's two Slavic neighbors, Ukraine and Belarus, have virtually no problems with different ethnic groups. Despite their abundant economic troubles, both countries seem politically stable and determined to succeed.

The Baltic states. The Baltic states, not so long ago dizzy from their newly won independence, are now facing the sobering reality of their economic difficulties. These hardships helped cause the defeat of the nationalist *Sajudis* movement in Lithuania in late 1992 and brought to power reform Communists who prefer a slower pace of economic reforms and friendlier relations with Russia.

Moldova. Little Moldova in the south has witnessed violence between its Slav population and the ethnically Romanian Moldovans. Fortunately, there appears to be enough determination on the part of Moldovan, Russian, and Ukrainian leaders to settle this conflict.

Transcaucasia. The violence that has beset Transcaucasia since the late 1980s shows no signs of letting up. The largest conflict involves Armenia and Azerbaijan, but there has also been much violence in Georgia and along the Georgian-Russian border involving small ethnic groups of Abkhazians, Ossetians, Chechen, and Ingushetians.

Central Asian Republics. Of the five central Asian republics, Kazakhstan has emerged as the most stable country, while Tajikistan has been convulsed by a violent civil war. All the republics are predominantly Muslim, but their leaders have repeatedly expressed preference for a "Turkish model" (moderate Islam and pluralism) rather than the fundamentalist form of government that rules Iran.

Two of the outstanding features of the Cold War were international political stability and clearly defined ideological and moral positions. The world is now a different place: more interconnected, more confusing, less predictable, and, some argue, much more dangerous. In this new world, however, let us hope that eventually those once enslaved by Communist regimes will learn to handle freedom responsibly—for their individual benefit and for the well-being of others.

INDEX

Abkhazia 49, 50, 67, 105
Afghanistan 20, 24, 28, 49, 50
Africa 6
Albania 6, 12, 50-51, 102, 104
  overview 16, 18, 20, 22, 24, 26, 34,
    36, 38, 40, 42, 44, 46
Albanians
  Kosovo 25, 29, 75
  refugees 40, 42, 44, 51
  Yugoslavia 23
Alia, Ramiz 22, 36, 38, 42, 51
Andropov, Yuri 22
Antall, Jozsef 39
Antisocialist 51
Armenia 32, 34, 42, 49, 52, 105
  earthquake 26
  Nagorny Karabakh 80
  Ter-Petrosyan, Levon 94
Armenians in Azerbaijan 26, 36, 52
Arms reduction 19, 20, 25, 48,
    56, 61
Arts 11-12
Azerbaijan 26, 32, 34, 36, 42,
    52, 61, 105
  Nagorny Karabakh 80
  overview 49
Baikonur space center 49, 74
Baltic Republics 30, 32, 34, 42, 48,
    52-53 see also Estonia; Latvia;
    Lithuania
Banking 10
Belarus 48, 53-54, 105
Berisha, Sali 46
Berlin 16, 17, 24
Berlin Wall 18, 34, 54
Black market 10
Black Sea Fleet 48, 61
Bosnia and Herzegovina 47, 54-55, 61,
    66, 98-99
Brandt, Willy 19, 55, 64, 66
Brazauskas, Algirdas 77
Brezhnev, Leonid 18, 20, 22,
    55-56, 64
Brezhnev Doctrine 18, 56
Bulgaria 56-57, 105
  Albania 24
  Marxism-Leninism 8
  overview 16, 20, 22, 24, 26, 30, 32,
    34, 36, 38, 40, 42, 44, 46
  Zhelev, Zhelyu 99
  Zhivkov, Todor 99
Bush, George 31, 35, 39, 45, 57
Carter, Jimmy 20
Castro, Fidel 3, 17
Ceauşescu, Elena 11, 21, 35
Ceauşescu, Nicolae 19, 21, 25, 27,
    35, 58, 103
  Marxism-Leninism 9
  Romania 87-88
Central Asia 103 see also names of
    countries
Charter 77 20, 24, 59, 63
Chechen 105
Chernenko, Konstantin 22
Chernobyl 22
Chevron investment in Kazakhstan 49, 74
China 6, 20, 49, 58-59
  student demonstrations 29
  United States 21
  U.S.S.R. 31
Churchill, Sir Winston 17, 72
Citizenship laws 48, 76
Civic Forum 38, 40, 42
Clinton, Bill 49
CMEA see COMECON
Cold War 16, 17, 57, 59-60
COMECON 16, 18, 60
Command economy 9-10

Commonwealth of Independent States
    44, 48, 60-61 see also names of
    countries
  Baikonur space center 74
Communism 61
  fall of 13-15
  Hungary 71
  Marxism-Leninism 78
  nomenclature 81, 102
  October Revolution 81
  origins and expansion 4-6
  personality cult 82
  restitutions and compensations 86
  revisionism 86
  societies under 7-12
Communist party 7-8, 103
Conference on Security and Cooperation
    in Europe 41, 61
Council for Mutual Economic
    Assistance see COMECON
Counterrevolutionary 17, 61
Crime 101
Crimea 61
Croatia 29, 39, 43, 44, 45, 61-62
  overview 47
  Tudjman, Franjo 94
  Vukovar 97
  Yugoslavia 98
Cuba 6, 17, 18, 62
Czechoslovakia 3, 62-63
  Charter 77 (manifesto) 59
  Havel, Václav 69-70
  Marxism-Leninism 8
  overview 16, 18, 20, 24, 26, 28, 30,
    32, 34, 36, 38, 40, 42, 46
  Prague Spring 84
  privatization 85
  religion 12
  secret police 103
  Warsaw Pact invasion 98
Czech Republic 62, 63, 74, 102,
    103, 105
De-Stalinization 16, 64
Détente 56, 64, 82
Dissident 64
  Charter 77 (manifesto) 59
  Czechoslovakia 28, 30
  East Germany 24
  Gamsakhurdia, Zviad K. 67
  Havel, Václav 69-70
  Sakharov, Andrei 88
  Solzhenitsyn, Aleksandr 92
Dnestr Republic 48, 64, 79, 100
Dubček, Alexander 18, 34, 46, 63,
    64-65, 91
Eastern Europe 6, 65 see also names of
    countries
East Germany 65-66, 105
  Brandt visit 19
  Honecker, Erich 70
  Hungarian border opening 71-72
  overview 16, 18, 20, 22, 24, 26, 28,
    32, 34, 36, 38, 40
  religion 12
  reunification with West Germany see
    Germany — reunification
  secret police 103
  "Shoot-to-kill" policy 90
  unemployment 42, 49
Ecology 103
Economy 9-10, 74, 101-2 see also
    individual countries
  European Bank for Reconstruction and
    Development 39
  price liberalization 84
  private enterprise 104
  privatization 85
Elchibev, Abulfaz 49

Estonia 26, 36, 38, 42, 44, 48, 66
Ethnic and political violence 2,
    14-15, 100-101, 105
  Abkhazia 50, 67
  Azerbaijan 26, 32, 36, 52
  Bosnia and Herzegovina 47, 55
  Bulgaria 22, 30, 32, 36
  Croatia 43, 45, 62
  Dnestr Republic 64
  ethnic cleansing 66
  Georgia 32, 67
  Germany 44
  Kazakhstan 30
  Kosovo 25, 29, 75
  Kyrgyzstan 75
  Moldova 79
  Nagorny Karabakh 80
  Ossetia 32, 48, 49, 81
  Romani 86-87
  Romania 27, 37
  Russia 48
  Sarajevo 89
  Serbia 89
  Slovakia 90-91
  Tajikistan 93-94
  Uzbekistan 30
  Yugoslavia 98-99
Ethnic cleansing 55, 66
European Bank for Reconstruction and
    Development 39
Few Sentences, A 30, 32
Gamsakhurdia, Zviad K. 42, 49,
    61, 67
Gdańsk 23, 27
Georgia 28, 32, 34, 42, 61, 67, 105
  Ossetia 81
  overview 49
  Shevardnadze, Eduard 89
Germany 41, 68-69 see also East
    Germany
  ecological damage 103
  overview 42, 44
  Poland 43
  refugees 85-86, 101
  reunification 36, 37, 40, 66, 74
  Romani 86
  U.S.S.R. 68-69
Gierek, Edward 19, 82
Glasnost 22, 69, 82
Gomuľka, Wľadysľaw 17, 82
Göncz, Árpád 41
Gorbachev, Mikhail 22, 24, 30, 36, 40,
    42, 44, 69
  Afghanistan 50
  Bush, meetings with 35, 39, 45
  China, visit to 31
  deposition attempt 14
  John Paul II, meeting with 34, 73,
  perestroika 82
  Reagan, meetings with 23, 25, 85
  resignation 61
  Romania, visit to 23
  Union of Soviet Socialist Republics 96
  Yugoslavia, visit to 25
Greece 42, 47, 51
Grósz, Károly 25, 27
Gypsies see Romani
Havel, Václav 28, 30, 34, 36, 40, 46,
    63, 69-70
Helsinki Accords 21, 61, 70
Honecker, Erich 22, 32, 49, 54, 66,
    70, 103
  "Shoot-to-kill" policy 90
  Soviet media, criticism of 26
  West Germany, visit to 24
Hoxha, Enver 6, 16, 22, 51
Human rights 11, 20, 21, 32, 70
Humor, political 12, 54

Hungarians in Romania 27, 37
Hungary 70-72
  Albania 26
  border opening 32
  Kádár, János 73
  Marxism-Leninism 8
  overview 17, 19, 21, 25, 27, 29, 31,
    33, 35, 37, 39, 41, 43, 45, 46
  refugees 85
Husák, Gustáv 18, 24, 34, 63
Iliescu, Ion 35, 39, 47, 72
Ingushetia 48, 105
Iraq 41
Iron Curtain 17, 72
Israel 18
Italy 42, 44
Izetbegović, Alija 47, 61, 72
Jakeš, Miloš 12, 24
Japan 48
Jaruzelski, Wojciech 21, 31, 73, 83
John Paul II 23, 34, 39, 43, 73
  assassination attempt 21, 22
  Poland 82
Kádár, János 17, 19, 25, 31,
  71, 73
Katyn Forest massacre 39
Kazakhstan 30, 48, 49, 73-74, 80
Kennedy, John F. 19
Kennedy, Robert 19
Khrushchev, Nikita 16, 18, 19,
  64, 74
Kim-Il Sun 75
King, Martin Luther, Jr. 19
Kiszczak, Czeslaw 27, 29
Klaus, Václav 40, 46, 74
Kohl, Helmut 24, 31, 35, 41,
  66, 74
Korea, North 3, 6, 75
Korean War 17
Kosovo 25, 29, 37, 41, 75
Kravchuk, Leonid 48, 61, 75
Krenz, Egon 32, 66
Krzysztof, Jan 43
Kuwait 41
Kyrgyzstan 49, 75-76
Landsbergis, Vytautas 76
Latvia 26, 36, 38, 42, 44, 48, 76
Lenin, Vladimir Ilich 4
Ligachev, Yegor 24, 76
Literature 12
Lithuania 34, 36, 38, 40, 42, 44, 48,
  76-77, 105
Macedonia 43, 47, 77
Mao Tse-Tung 58-59
Markovic, Ante 29, 77
Marx, Karl 4, 12
Marxism-Leninism 8-9, 78
Mass media 11
Mazowiecki, Tadeusz 32, 41,
  78, 83
Mečiar, Vladimir 42, 46, 78,
  90-91, 104
Michael (king of Romania) 27, 39
Milošević, Slobodan 14, 47,
  79, 104
Mladenov, Petur 34, 38, 40
Modrow, Hans 34, 36
Moldavia see Moldova
Moldova 38, 48, 79, 91, 100, 105
  Romania 47
Mongolia 3, 6, 49, 79
Montenegro 47
Mutalibov, Ayaz N. 49, 52
Nabiyev, Rakhman 49, 80, 94, 101
Nagorny Karabakh 24, 28, 34, 49,
  52, 80
Nagy, Imre 17, 31
Najibullah 49
Nakhichevan 52
NATO 17, 47, 74, 80
Navrátil, Augustin 24
Nazarbayev, Nursultan 74, 80
Németh, Miklós 27
New Forum 32, 34
Nicaragua 37, 80

Nixon, Richard 20, 21, 64
Nobel Peace Prize
  Brandt, Willy 55
  Gorbachev, Mikhail 69
  Sakharov, Andrei 88
  Wałęsa, Lech 23, 97
Nomenclature 7-8, 81, 102
North Atlantic Treaty Organization see
  NATO
October Revolution 81
Olszewski, Jan 45
Ossetia 32, 48, 49, 67, 81, 105
Ostpolitik 55, 66
Panić, Milan 47, 81
Peace Corps 48
Perestroika 22, 76, 82
Personality cult 42, 82, 93
Poland 82-84, 105
  ecological damage 103
  Jaruzelski, Wojciech 73
  Marxism-Leninism 8
  Mazowiecki, Tadeusz 78
  overview 17, 19, 21, 23, 25, 27, 29,
    31, 33, 35, 37, 39, 41, 43, 45, 46
  religion 12
  Solidarity 92
  Wałęsa, Lech 97
Police, secret 8, 103
Popieluszko, Jerzy 23
Pószgay, Imre 29
Prague Spring 18, 63, 84
Price liberalization 48, 84
  Poland 25, 46
  Romania 43
  Uzbekistan 49
Private enterprise 104
Privatization 85
  Czechoslovakia 46
  Romania 47
  Russia 48
Radio 12
Radio Free Europe 12
Radio Liberty 12
Reagan, Ronald 21, 23, 25, 85
Refugees 85-86, 101
  Albania 40
  Bosnia and Herzegovina 47
  Croatia 62
  Greece 42
  Hungary 62
  Italy 42, 44
  Turkey 32
Religion 12, 24, 26
Restitutions and compensations 86, 103-4
  Czechoslovakia 42
  Hungary 43
Revisionism 86
Roman, Petre 47, 86
Romani 86-87
Romania 58, 87-88, 105
  ecological damage 103
  Hungarian minority 27, 37
  Iliescu, Ion 72
  Marxism-Leninism 8
  overview 17, 19, 21, 23, 25, 27, 29,
    31, 33, 35, 37, 39, 41, 43, 45, 47
  Roman, Petré 86
Russia 4, 38, 48, 88, 105
  Black Sea Fleet 61
  Ossetia 81
Sajudis 76, 77, 105
Sakharov, Andrei 28, 30, 34, 88
SALT agreements 20, 56
Sarajevo 47, 55, 89
Schmidt, Helmut 20
Secret police 8, 103
Serbia 35, 41, 45, 47, 89
  Kosovo 75
  Milošević, Slobodan 79
Shevardnadze, Eduard 40, 49, 67,
  81, 89
"Shoot-to-kill" (policy) 42, 90
Sinatra Doctrine 32, 90
Six-Day-War 19
Slovakia 36, 38, 40, 78, 90-91, 105

Slovenia 29, 35, 37, 45, 91
  independence 33, 43, 44
  overview 47
Snegur, Mircea 79, 91, 104
Socialism 4, 12, 91
Society, Communist 10-12, 104
Solidarity 21, 23, 27, 29, 31, 33, 39,
  92
  Poland 82-83, 84
Solzhenitsyn, Aleksandr 20, 92-93
Soviet Union see Union of Soviet
  Socialist Republics
Stalin, Joseph 4, 16, 73, 93, 100
  de-Stalinization 64
  Georgia 67
  personality cult 82
  socialism 91
Stasi 103
Stoph, Willi 18
Strougal, Lubomír 26
Suchocka, Hanna 46
Tajikistan 49, 80, 93-94, 101
Television 12
Ter-Petrosyan, Levon 94
Theater 12
Tito, Josip Broz 6, 17, 94, 98
Tökes, Lázsló 35
Transcaucasia see names of countries
Trans-Dniester Republic see Dnestr
  Republic
Travel 11
Tudjman, Franjo 47, 94
Turkmenistan 94
Turks 22, 30, 32, 36, 50, 67
Ukraine 30, 32, 40, 45, 48, 94-95, 105
  Black Sea Fleet 61
  Kravchuk, Leonid 75
Ulbricht, Walter 16, 65
Union of Soviet Socialist Republics
  95-96
  Albania 18
  Hungary 37
  overview 16, 18, 20, 22, 24, 26, 28,
    30, 32, 34, 36, 38, 40, 42, 44
  Yugoslavia 17
United Nations
  Croatia 47, 62
  ethnic cleansing, resolution on 47, 66
  Sarajevo 47, 89
  Yugoslavia 47, 99
United States 96
  China 21
  Cuba 18, 19
  Kazakhstan oil-field development 74
  Korean War 17
  Peace Corps aids Moscow 48
  Vietnam 19, 97
U.S.S.R. see Union of Soviet Socialist
  Republics
Uzbekistan 30, 38, 49, 97
Uzbeks in Kyrgyzstan 75
Velvet Revolution 63, 70
Vietnam 6, 19, 21, 97
Vukovar 45, 97
Wałęsa, Lech 21, 23, 27, 29,
  31, 41, 43, 97
  Poland 84
  Solidarity 92
Warsaw Pact 16, 18, 31, 32, 44, 98
Yalta Conference 4, 16
Yeltsin, Boris 14, 24, 28, 33, 38, 40,
  42, 44, 48, 61, 98
  Baltic Republics 53
  Ossetia 81
Yugoslavia 3, 6, 98-99, 105
  Markovic, Ante 77
  overview 17, 19, 21, 23, 25, 29, 33,
    35, 37, 39, 41, 43, 45, 47
  Panić, Milan 81
  refugees 51, 85
  revisionism 86
  Tito, Josip Broz 94
Zhelev, Zhelyu 40, 46, 57, 99
Zhivkov, Todor 34, 46, 57, 99, 103
Zhivkova, Lyudmila 20

ILLUSTRATION CREDITS

The following list acknowledges, according to page, the sources of illustrations used in LANDS AND PEOPLES SPECIAL EDITION: LIFE AFTER COMMUNISM. The credits are listed illustration by illustration — top to bottom, left to right. When the name of the photographer has been listed with the source, the two are separated by a slash. If two or more illustrations appear on the same page, their credits are separated by semicolons.

2	© Van Morvan/Sygma	49	© B. Markel/Gamma-Liaison
6	© UPI		© Swersey/Gamma-Liaison
7	© Keystone	50	© Francois Lehr/Sipa Press
8	© Jose Nicolas/Sipa Press	53	© Laski/Sipa Press
9	© Christian Valdes/Lehtikuva Oy/Saba	54	© Anthony Suau/Black Star
13	© Thierry Chesnot/Sipa Press	55	UPI
15	© Tania Makeeva/Sipa Press	56	© Patrick Forestier
16	© UPI; © Erich Lessing; © UPI	57	© B. Markel/Gamma-Liaison
17	International News Photos	58	© William Stevens/Gamma-Liaison
18	Paris Match; AP/Wide World Photos	59	© Chine Nouvelle/Sipa Press
19	© UPI	61	© V. Kiselyov/Lehtikuva/Woodfin Camp & Assoc.
20	© Both photos: © UPI		
21	© Sygma; © UPI; © Keler/Sygma	62	© Reuters/Bettmann
22	© Roland Neveu/Gamma-Liaison; AP/Wide World Photos	63	© Frederico Mendes/Sipa Press
		65	© Orban/Sygma
23	© UPI; © Ed Wojtas © David Burnett/Contact	67	© Antoine Gyori/Sygma
		68	© Robert Wallis/Sipa Press
24	AP/Wide World Photos	69	© A. Nogues/Sygma
26	© Laski/Sipa; AP/Wide World Photos	70	© Chesnot/Sipa Press
27	© Kok/Gamma-Liaison	71	© Shepard Sherbell/Saba
28	AP/Wide World Photos	72	© Francois Lehr/Sipa Press
30	© Yankelevitch/Sipa Press	73	© Jeremy Nicholl/Katz/Saba
31	© Sygma	74	© Pierre Adenis/Sipa Press
33	© Shepard Sherbell/Saba; © D. Hudson/Sygma	75	© Thierry Chesnot/Sipa Press
		76	© T. Veermae/Lehtikuva/Saba
34	© Witt/Sipa	77	© Reuters/Bettmann
35	© Luc Delahaye/Sipa; AP/Wide World Photos	78	© Sygma
		79	© Serge Sibert/Matrix
37	© A. Nogues/Sygma	80	© Wesley Bocxe/Sipa Press
38	© Alexandra Avakian/Woodfin Camp & Assoc.	81	© L. Delahaye/Sipa Press
		83	© Jurgen Vogt/The Image Bank
39	© Frederic Stevens/Sipa Press	84	© A. Solomonov/RIA/Sipa Press
40	© J. Langevin/Sygma	85	© Tass from Sovfoto
41	© Chip Hires/Gamma-Liaison; © Wojteck Laski/Sipa Press	86	© Filip Horvat/Saba
		87	© Luc Delahaye/Sipa Press
42	© Chris Niedenthal/Black Star	89	© Francoise Demulder/Sipa Press
43	© Delahaye/Sipa Press © Pocius/Sygma	90	© UPI/Bettmann
		91	© AP/Wide World Photos
44	© Roberto Koch/Saba © Tilt Vermae/Lehtikuva/Saba © Rudiger Schilight Stern/Black Star	92	© B. Bisson/Sygma
		93	Signal Corps/Acme
		94	© Reuters/Bettmann
45	© Jean-Claude Coutausse/Contact/ Woodfin Camp & Assoc. © Filip Horvat/Saba	95	© P. Le Segretain/Sygma
		97	© Jeffrey Markowitz/Sygma
		99	© Peter Turnley/Black Star
46	© J. Langevin/Sygma © Paul Miller/Black Star © Reuters/Bettman	100	© Demulder/Sipa Press
		101	© Peter Turnley/Black Star
		102	© R. Bossu/Sygma
47	© Reuters/Bettman © Paul Herve/Sipa Press	103	© Dorigny/REA/Saba
		104	© A. Solomonov/Ria Novosti/Sipa Press
48	© East News/Sipa Press		

Cover and title page photo: © Peter Turnley/Black Star
Contents page photos: © Tania Makeeva/Sipa Press; © Pocius/Sygma; © Francoise Demulder/Sipa Press; © Peter Turnley/Black Star